The Blue Room

The Blue Room

Trauma and Testimony among Refugee Women
A psycho-social exploration

Inger Agger

Translated by Mary Bille

Zed Books Ltd
London and New Jersey

The Blue Room was first published in Danish under the title
Det Blå Værelse, by Hans Reitzels Forlag, Copenhagen, in 1992.
First published in English by Zed Books Ltd, 7 Cynthia Street,
London N1 9JF, UK, and 165 First Avenue, Atlantic Highlands,
New Jersey 07716, USA, in 1994

Cover designed by Andrew Corbett.
Typeset by EMS Photosetters, Thorpe Bay, Essex.
Printed and bound in the United Kingdom
by Biddles Ltd, Guildford and King's Lynn.

A catalogue record for this book is
available from the British Library

US CIP data is available
from the Library of Congress

ISBN 1 85649 239 7 Hb
ISBN 1 85649 240 0 Pb

Contents

1. In The Blue Room

This is a narrative about boundaries. About bodily, psychological, cultural, social and political boundaries. It is a narrative about barriers that are overcome – about crossing borders and having your boundaries violated – and about being in the ambiguous borderland where you have *to be careful* of your own, other people's and the system's boundaries.

In *The Blue Room*, 40 different stories are told, but gradually I come to hear them as a single testimony of one sex's painful struggle to extend its space – to move the boundaries of the permissible and fight the power of shame. But it is also testimony about what can happen when you try to move the frontier: those in power will not surrender their territory voluntarily.

This is a women's narrative in the sense that it tells about women's lives and their struggle against boundaries that are too limiting. And even though this narrative grows out of the meeting with refugee women from distant countries in the Middle East and Latin America, its theme is also universal: oppression and rebellion and the necessity of moving frontiers even when the struggle inflicts wounds that can never be completely healed. With this narrative, I attempt to describe some of the methods used by those in power in much of the world to control and punish women who threaten the system's boundaries, women who are socially and politically dangerous. Sexuality plays an important role in these control–and–punish methods, and the narrative describes the traumatic consequences of these methods, consequences that affect the woman, herself, her love relationships and her political commitment. I attempt, furthermore, to deepen our understanding of the dynamics of the trauma that can result from political 'discipline'. I try especially to relate to the problem of *complicity*: that paradoxical, shameful feeling of being an accessory which can arise in the person whose boundaries have been violated.

With both the narrative's form and content, I attempt to illustrate a possible healing process: the narrative is placed inside a ritual space, a 'women's house of exile', in which testimony about 'the evil' can be given and possibly transformed into insight and a new commitment. But with this narrative I also attempt to deepen the understanding of sexual trauma in general and of women's position in particular.

Women are to a great extent controlled in connection with their reproductive functions; therefore, it is possible for them to create a crisis in society – through 'sexual' rebellion (Goddard 1987). Silence and invisibility are important elements in women's special status (Ardener 1989). So anything can happen if women leave their houses, move out into society, speak out and become visible, if they move into the public space and thereby invade men's territory, if they are not *careful*, but bring disorder and impurity into society (Douglas 1966). This special status in relation to those in power is not necessarily impotent; on the contrary, it can be an excellent basis for rebellion. The oppressed also represent a threat, and women's role in marking the boundaries of the system can be especially important in critical situations when the system's survival is threatened (Goddard 1987).

We can thus also see exile as an existential situation for women who wish to abandon their silent and invisible lives in an androcentric culture. But in addition to the gender-determined conditions, other conditions can be woven into and reinforce this position. Membership of political, ethnic or religious groups that are considered threatening or 'abnormal' by the political power holders can also provoke oppression. Both women and men belonging to such groups can become victims of persecution, rape, imprisonment, torture, murder, deportation, exile, an existence as refugee – everything we call 'organized violence' (van Geuns 1987). Both active and passive members of such groups can become victims of this organized violence: active, politically conscious people who work systematically to change the existing power relations, or people who just belong to a particular ethnic group, for example, or belong to the same family as one who is politically active in an oppositional group. Women who participate in such groups commit a double crime: they both move out of the private sphere of their homes into public space and threaten the masculine territory, and they challenge the political power. The strategy of those in power toward such women is also double: they are punished both as dangerous women and as threatening political opponents.

The name I have chosen for the narrative is *The Blue Room*. With this metaphorical title, I want to direct attention to the issues of ritual space, gender, testimony, trauma and victimization. In this opening chapter, I first introduce the ritual space of The Blue Room, a space which I created both during my interviews with the refugee women and during my own subsequent writing process. Next, I comment on gender-specific abuse of women – that is, the topic of human rights violations against women. Thereafter, I outline some of the ways I have used the women's testimony in the ritual space of The Blue Room. I focus on some issues connected with sexual trauma and victimization, especially with regard to the problem of complicity and to the power of shame, and lastly, I introduce you to the women in The Blue Room.

My point of departure is a concept of human rights based on the United Nations Universal Declaration of 1948. Hereby, I take an ethical, non-neutral position. This perspective focuses on universal cross-cultural rights. In the case of refugee women, it directs attention to common aspects instead of different cultural contexts. Moreover, the ethical dimension of this concept of universal human rights also has implications for the healing process: it places guilt outside the victim, and also forces the witness (helper, therapist, researcher) to take a moral stand. Thus, the concept of human rights can be an eye-opener for both victims and witnesses. For many who have suffered human rights violations, it will come as a surprise that they have any rights at all and that the international community has agreed on their right to a dignified life. This knowledge in itself can be a first step in a process of consciousness-raising or post-traumatic therapy. An awareness of the ethical dimensions of the human rights concept can also mark the beginning of a consciousness-raising process for the witness–therapist–researcher.

The ritual space of the Blue Room

I had worked for five years as a therapist for traumatized refugees when I decided that I needed to process some of my experiences through theoretical work and research. The project I planned was directly connected with my previous work. It was motivated by a need to understand some of the strange and terrifying experiences my female patients had told me about: more specifically, the role of sexuality in political persecution. But it was also motivated by a need to 'rid' myself of some of the evil I, as a therapist, had to contain. I wished to give meaning to the incredible stories I had heard, by reframing them, and I also wished to give my own testimony of how it is to meet deliberate human evil.

This narrative, however, not only originates in these years of clinical 'field work'. In my private and professional search for 'the healing', I have carried out field work in such different ritual spaces as the consciousness-raising groups of the women's movement at the start of the 1970s, the therapy movement that followed with its alternative and authorized group forms, and the solidarity movement's travellers to Latin America and the East. Work as a clinical therapist for traumatized political refugees was only a natural step along a path which started long before and was guided by an effort to find directions in my work that could enhance an understanding of how private and political levels interact.

The research project involved interviews with traumatized refugee women. When the women told me their life stories, I was unavoidably confronted once more with the therapist's problem of containing the trauma story even though I was now in the position of researcher. For one thing, since I could not just forget my clinical background, I was there – in the room, The Blue Room – both as therapist and researcher. Secondly, my clinical background was valuable for the interview process, because it gave me the knowledge and courage to enter into difficult parts of the trauma story which were important to document, from a theoretical and political point of view.

So what did I do? I attempted to create a ritual space which I have called 'The Blue Room'. The Blue Room was the domain of my work. It was in this space my field work was carried out; it was here the women told me their stories; and it was here I wrote my narrative. It is both a totally real room in my apartment, with blue walls, but it also symbolizes the healing space in which two people, two cultures, two worlds can meet.

Here, I met the 40 women who came from ten different countries, and here they gave their testimony. In this room, each woman and I temporarily created a space together which, inspired by the anthropologist Kirsten Hastrup (1986), I have called 'a third culture'. We came from different cultures, but in The Blue Room we established something new and different to which we both contributed. It was in this new context that the story was told by her and heard by me.

The stories of The Blue Room are organized into a series of 'rooms' in a women's house of exile. The house and its rooms are seen as spaces in which the trauma stories can be integrated. The rooms are each fragments of a universe in a woman's world of exile, and each and all of them together contain different dimensions of a woman's life. And in a woman's life, some of the most important defining spaces relate to sexuality and reproduction. Women define themselves and are defined in relation to their reproductive function to a much greater degree than men. The context of women's lives has for centuries, maybe millennia, been bound to the responsibility for giving and nourishing life (Brun 1991).

With the women's house of exile, therefore, I am trying to invent and define a certain social and psychological space (Clifford & Marcus 1986) in which a psychological transformation can take place. I seek, in other words, to draw a map and give a name to some specific areas of significance for the refugee woman's world. For the 'map is not the territory, and the name is not the thing named' (Bateson & Bateson 1988, p. 21).

By drawing this particular map, I am trying to catch some common traits in the different stories, and I have the opportunity to 'cross-cut' the stories and describe both the trauma and the healing on a multi-dimensional plane. By placing the individual rooms in a certain relation to each other, I also have an opportunity to describe a process.

The stories of The Blue Room are about life in the girl's childhood, and about the prison cells the women were led to. They are stories about daily life in exile. Thus, it is not my purpose here to prove what 'really' happened. In meeting with the women and their testimonies, I experienced that what the women told me was true, but how could I ever 'prove' it? There is a general mistrust of victims' stories; no one wants to know about the 'unspeakable' (Herman 1992). It is this mistrust which is exploited by dictatorships when they deny that they abuse human rights.

So the stories of The Blue Room belong to the women, and carry with them their owners' rebellion, trauma, and sources of healing. Stories can become narratives when they are told to a solitary witness; therefore, it is important to tell each other stories. Narratives are expanded metaphors, and we can use narratives just as we use metaphors – to think with. Or rather: we think in narratives, as anthropologist Gregory Bateson expresses it (1988). But just as metaphors and narratives create insight, the narration can also have transforming power. Some stories are so disturbing that they *must* be told in order for them to lose their destructive power. One of the most important elements in a healing process is to come to possess your own story and thereby create your own narrative. Poets have always known this.

In the healing process, material which lies deep within the inner world can be given a space, can be transformed or consolidated through the therapist's correct use of metaphors. Metaphors do not threaten to invade or penetrate a defence from without, but are experienced instead as a growing inner strength (Cox & Theilgaard 1987).

The exile house we are in now is thus one of the houses inhabited by women who have been rejected by the system from which they both come and have rebelled against. Like other houses for exiles, it lies on the periphery and its inhabitants are marginal. Their voices tell us about the forces that struggle in the borderland. The women's house of exile and its rooms can therefore be seen as spaces within which the feminine aspects of life can both be told and de-privatized. The house and its rooms thus become metaphors that can transpose and expand the meaning of the individual stories.

Metaphors are appropriate for expressing intuitive knowledge, and the use of metaphors and symbols is characteristic for the threshold phase in a ritual process (Turner 1974). By using metaphors, I thus also bring into the foreground the sense of fellowship, or what Turner calls the *communitas* aspect of ritual.

This feeling of fellowship is equally important for victim and witness. How do we therapists, researchers, readers who become witnesses react when confronted with horrifying stories about deliberate, man-made, human rights violations? How do we, supposedly the victims' helpers, contain their stories and simultaneously manage our own pain? We witness d girls who have experienced gender-specific human rights ... – be it refugee women who have been sexually abused in prison or ..., flight, or in our own culture victims of rape, wife battering, incest or ...titution. We, the witnesses, are therefore confronted with the problem of how to create a space which also enables us to heal ourselves, a space which allows a victim to become a survivor, and the therapist or researcher to convert her own pain into a pro-social struggle.

An important tool in creating the ritual space of The Blue Room was the tape recorder. I began each interview by asking the woman to say her name, her age and her country into the tape recorder; then I stopped it and played back the tape. Together, we confirmed that the woman's voice was recorded and could be heard in The Blue Room. After that, she knew that *her* voice and *her* name could be heard. We were ready to start recording her testimony.

After the interview process was finished I was alone in The Blue Room with my collection of trauma stories. It was now up to me to write my narrative and my testimony of what I had seen, heard, thought and felt. I chose to expand the ritual space of The Blue Room into the written text by using two key metaphors: rooms in a house and boundaries between spaces. The Blue Room was the space in which the interviews took place and gave its name to this first chapter of my narrative. The title of each of the following chapters is a different room: The Daughter's Room, The Father's Room, The Cell, The Mother's Room, The Living Room and On the Veranda. They each represent a specific dimension of experience and relationships in the women's lives. But if the metaphor of rooms provides the narrative structure, the metaphor of boundaries, especially crossing boundaries, expresses the danger lurking in the lives of the women interviewed.

One of my main objectives was to understand how violence against women inside the prison is connected with the sexual–political power structure *outside* the prison. I try to clarify this connection both through the order in which the various rooms in the house are placed, and in the significance I give to each room. Each room is defined by a physical, psychological, social and historical dimension. By using these metaphoric spaces, I attempt to capture the relevant aspects of all these dimensions at the same time, rather than trying to find any simple or mechanical cause-and-effect explanation; instead, I want to reach a deeper understanding of how the different dimensions influence each other and create the field I have chosen to make the object of my investigation (Jensen 1992).

From The Blue Room we travel backward in time and forward again toward daily life in the present. But we also leap downward in an inner psychological process toward the darkest sides of existence, toward the areas where we can encounter sexuality and aggression in their most dangerous and threatening aspects. From this voyage we surface again with the discoveries we have made; and with The Blue Room's insight, we can perhaps use these discoveries to make a new beginning. We emerge from the tunnel with a longing for change, bringing with us the new insight which must first be anchored on the other side of the darkness.

In the final chapter, therefore, On the Veranda, I create a metaphorical healing circle. Here, I let the voices of the women speak to each other, and suggest that one important tool for healing is for victims to gather together in such ritual spaces as a way of giving testimony in a context of compassion and understanding.

My narrative style uses metaphorical language as a way of expressing my own wish to integrate what I have heard and sensed. A process of splitting, of dissociation, between thoughts and feelings is one of the cardinal symptoms of trauma. As metaphors integrate thoughts and feelings, I thus attempt to write about trauma in a less 'dissociated' language. Speaking about the unspeakable without emotional involvement is another way of denying reality. Thus, the experimental narrative style was chosen as a personally felt necessity.

Gender-specific abuse

My point of departure for the meeting in The Blue Room is the wish 'to name' the special violence which is practised against politically dangerous women. For this purpose, it is important to understand how the social and political discipline of women is effected through their sexuality. It is a discipline seen in its most revealing form in the sexual violence against women political prisoners. The consequences of the violence – the sexual trauma and the power of shame – must be understood if we are to find better strategies for healing. In 1985, Eva Forest, from her experience with women political prisoners in Spain, wrote that it could be important to study the sexual violence practised against women in prisons. From a new and revealing perspective, this could make it possible to analyse some structural aspects of our own society. Prominent in my understanding of trauma after violence against women has been that: the forms of oppression carried out against women in general and politically dangerous women in particular, must be understood in relation to the existing sexual–political power structure.

In connection with my clinical work, both through reading reports from Latin America (especially Lira & Weinstein 1986; Weinstein & Lira 1987) and through meeting refugee women who had been in prison, I discovered that almost all women political prisoners are subjected to sexual assault of one kind or another. This subject, however, was apparently more or less taboo, as incest and rape had been earlier. It was, therefore, important to contribute to making it visible and speakable, to name this political use of sexuality in the service of repression.

In its traumatic consequences, its confusing ambiguity resembles other forms of sexual assault. When aggression and sexuality are intertwined, it is especially difficult to maintain a psychological defence, particularly to defend yourself against the sense of shame at being an accomplice to the forbidden deed; this can threaten the innermost, most central part of your identity. The widespread use of sexual assault against political prisoners can, therefore, be seen as an effective strategy if the aim is to break down a political opponent's personal identity – and thereby also her *political* identity (Agger & Jensen 1989; Agger & Jensen 1993a, 1993b).

At the world congress on sexology in 1987, my contribution on sexual torture of women political prisoners was placed under the theme, 'anthropology, sex in the media' (Agger 1987), and I experienced how the taboo character of the subject could privately mark as questionable the researcher who wished to make such a subject open to discussion. As noted by Judith Herman (1992, p. 2), 'to speak publicly about one's knowledge of atrocities is to invite the stigma that attaches to victims . . . , as though contaminated by contact' (Ibid. p. 8). At the world congress in 1991, however, the subject had become more 'deprivatized' and recognized as a relevant research area within sexology. 'Sexual violence, torture and political power' was an official theme of the congress, and Amnesty International has published a book on sexual violence against politically active women (1991).

Today, the subject is of relevance in many parts of the world. Violations of women's human rights are widespread. Rather than diminishing, it is a growing problem encountered in both the north and the south. In Tanzania, for example, it is common to spread rumours that women political leaders are prostitutes; this rumour-mongering can be seen as an important element in the effort to hinder women's entrance into the public space (Andersen 1992). In connection with Iraq's invasion of Kuwait, a large number of Kuwaiti women were raped as part of the occupation force's strategy of conquest, and the impurity inflicted on these women has marked them and their families with such shame that they risk banishment (Weisaeth 1991). From another part of the world, we hear, for example, of the sexual assault against Tibetan women imprisoned by the Chinese occupation forces. This is at present a common procedure for humiliation as part of political repression (Mathiasen & Lützer 1992). In former Yugoslavia, a European Commission investigative mission concluded that mass rape of women is a systematic weapon used in warfare:

The mission accepted the view that rape is part of a pattern of abuse, usually perpetrated with the conscious intention of demoralizing and terrorizing communities, driving them from their home regions and demonstrating the power of the invading forces. (Warburton 1993, p. 5)

The testimony

All the women of The Blue Room had suffered human rights violations. Some had been imprisoned and tortured, others had close relatives who had been tortured or murdered. After arrival in Denmark, many had lived for months in refugee camps anxiously waiting for asylum to be granted.

In the meeting with the refugee women in The Blue Room, I used *testimony* as a research method. Thus, I attempted to unite my experience from the use of testimony in the consciousness-raising groups of the women's movement with experiences from my therapeutic training and my work with testimony as a trans-cultural therapeutic method. The use of this method implies that research and therapeutic processes are not separable. For victims of human rights violations, testimony has a special significance, because it becomes a documented accusation and a piece of evidence against the repressive system. 'Testimony' as a concept has a special, double connotation: it contains objective, judicial, public and political aspects as well as subjective, spiritual, cathartic and private aspects. Testimony thus contains the quality of uniting within its structure the private and the political levels (Agger & Jensen 1990).

In Chile during the dictatorship, testimonies were used for registering and denouncing extreme examples of torture. The victim's story was taped, transcribed and sent to international organizations as evidence against the dictatorship. Little by little the therapeutic value of the method also became evident and started a series of reflections on possibilities and limitations of the method for the healing of emotional sequels of torture. The psychologists Eugenia Weinstein and Elizabeth Lira (1987) observed that giving testimony alleviated symptoms, that it transformed something painful into a document which could be useful to other people. It was not only cathartic but was also a political and legal weapon against the aggressors. In this way, some of the aggression which the abuse had created in the victim could be channelled and elaborated in a socially constructive manner, whereby the self-destructive spiral was broken. 'It is a paradox', Weinstein and Lira add, 'that the testimony in some ways is a complete confession – that which they tried to extract by means of torture and which the subject protected at the cost of his or her pain. But now it is an act which is inscribed in the original existential project. The information will not be used against the comrades, but, rather, against the torturers' (Ibid. p. 67).

In general, this method was useful when you needed to confirm reality as a reality lived and experienced by a lot of people, and you needed also to communicate feelings, facts and give it into the hands of the people, of the person, as an instrument that could be used, if he or she needed it. The most important thing was to confirm the reality and also to avoid people having to tell the same story again and again. People had the story in their hands, and they could photocopy it and send it, and so on. It is very destroying to have to repeat and repeat your story because you are denouncing it – but in a dissociated way, without linking emotions with facts. This only produces a deeper dissociation. (Interview with Elizabeth Lira, in Agger & Jensen 1993b.)

As testimony, the traumatic story can thus be integrated and perhaps also given new meaning: the private shame can be transformed to political dignity. It can therefore become a source of new knowledge about the methods of the dictatorship, and at the same time heal the wounds inflicted through these methods.

The refugee women in my research project were nearly all visible, politically active women. They were well-educated and highly motivated to tell of conditions in their homelands. They could express and explain, vividly and sensitively, the circumstances of their own lives and also of their silent sisters who lived under poorer conditions. Through their testimonies, I tried to understand how the disciplinary punishment of politically active women is connected with the surrounding sexual and political power-structure and with the historically transmitted definitions of 'the shameful', and 'the unclean'. This could, I thought, add to the understanding of the problem of *complicity*.

In my narrative I have taken parts of individual women's stories and placed them within the different, relevant rooms. In one room, there can be small or large parts or several parts of a single story. In each room, the women's statements are placed within a theoretical framework. The most important aim has been to illuminate each room's theme with as many nuances as possible.

In the first room, The Blue Room, the actual meeting with the women takes place on the physical, psychological and social level; but the meeting is also influenced by the historical conditions we all carry with us. The Blue Room is a room in exile, and this also plays a decisive role in forming the story of the past. The story is told with an insight that is influenced by this country of exile (Denmark) and by my presence as a Danish woman. In this room, I define the field in which the stories are told, and from here the narrative begins and finds its form. From this room of insight, we go back to a series of spaces in the past.

The first space is the Daughter's Room, which is defined by the girl's physical development into a woman, her psychological reaction to that development and the control reactions her development calls forth from the surroundings. In this room she begins to learn about the problem of complicity and the power of shame. From here we enter the Father's Room, where the girl, both physically and psychologically, meets the man's world where her own sexual boundaries can be transgressed. She learns gradually that because of the historically transmitted patterns of meaning she herself is responsible for *being careful* that others do not transgress her boundaries.

The next space, The Cell, is the decisive scene of this narrative. In The Cell she meets organized political violence, and this meeting is the concrete reason for her being in The Blue Room as a political refugee. The Daughter's Room and the Father's Room are universes that almost all women enter in various local variations. In these spaces, power, control and violence are practised almost unconsciously as part of the social structure. And even though the experiences within these spaces have contributed to the development of the political consciousness of many of the women in The Blue Room, meeting with the political violence of state terrorism is qualitatively different, because the violence here is also practised consciously and systematically. And in The Cell she feels in her body and soul how the power of shame which she has already internalized can be exploited.

From this turning point of death and darkness, we enter a space which is defined by her relationship to new life – to her children. Here in The Mother's Room, we try to understand how political persecution influences the woman's relation to the child she is carrying in her body and to giving birth. Within this space the psychological conflict between her identity as mother and her identity as political activist is enacted; and in this space her relation to her children during flight and in exile is developed. From here we are unavoidably led into The Living Room, where the daily life of exile is reflected in the woman's physical and psychological reactions to her husband or lover, to the father of her children. Within this space the relationship to the man is developed under conditions that are determined by what has happened in the past, but also by the longing to return home or to find a new home.

After this voyage to the rooms of the past, we reach a space of the 'present', The Veranda. Here, I attempt to invent and define a psychological and social space, in which the traumatic story could be integrated and healed; and to anchor the insight from The Blue Room and the voyage through the rooms of the past in a process that develops among the women on The Veranda. With the ritual process of this space I try to create a transition to life outside a women's house of exile even though this house and its rooms will also remain part of us.

Sexual trauma and victimization

How can the trauma that ensues after serious human rights violations be characterized in general terms? We can understand the dynamics of the trauma from the perspectives of dissociation and victimization. The process of *dissociation* refers mainly to the victim's relationship to herself, that is, to the mechanisms of defence which are employed in the confrontation with the threat to life and the exposure to injury. The process of *victimization* refers mainly to the victim's relationship to others. This process describes the victim's reactions to the complex structure of the sexual abuse, especially in confrontation with the moral dilemmas and impossible choices to which she is exposed. Victimization, therefore, implies profound changes of ideological perspective and relates to the victim's relationship to the world and to her life project.

'So you turn yourself off – you dissociate', a Chilean psychiatrist told me about her psychological state during torture. 'What I lived through during my own experience of torture was something inconceivable which I could not contain' (Agger & Jensen 1993b). This process of 'turning yourself off', of dissociating, has an emotional and a cognitive dimension. It is an ego-defence process which involves splitting and repression (Lifton 1988; Wilson 1989). Lira (1983) describes the traumatic experience as something which becomes split off and encapsulated in the psychological world of the victim. The magnitude of damage spreading from this encapsulated experience will depend on external and internal factors: the degree of continued persecution by the dictatorship after release from prison, and the emotional significance attached to the abuse by the victim and her primary social group – family, colleagues and political comrades.

Weinstein and Lira (1987) emphasize that the process of dissociation is central in understanding a person's experience during torture and that a dissociative process is also an essential part of the subsequent reactions to the trauma. Dissociation is a means of psychological survival during torture, they claim: by dissociating, the victim establishes a partial disintegration of his or her ego in order to avoid an overwhelming anxiety which would lead to total disintegration. *'This happened to me as an object, not as a subject'* (Ibid. p. 49). Lifton (1988) has described this defence mechanism as extreme *psychic numbing*, or as a form of self-hypnosis. Judith Herman (1992) relates how the 'dialectics of trauma' are characterized by an alternation between numbness and reliving the event. Dissociation as a mode of psychological survival when confronted with the impossible choice between bodily or emotional integrity, leads the victim to create a split inside herself (Weinstein & Lira 1987) and thus also to feel that she participates in her own disintegration.

McCann and Pearlman (1990, p. 41) define dissociation as a cognitive disturbance that is characterized by 'an alteration of consciousness in which experiences and affects are not integrated into memory and awareness'. They add that depersonalization, derealization and fragmentation are symptoms of dissociation in connection with severe childhood abuse, and the split-off memory fragments can exist as 'a hidden self that remembers the abuse and may be continuing to protect the adult self through the dissociative process' (ibid. p. 286).

Apparently, there are a number of similarities between the dynamics of traumata after incest and political torture. Weinstein and Lira (1987, p. 49) use the terms 'indifference' ('I felt like an object') and 'unreality' ('it was like a nightmare') about the emotional state of the victim both during and after torture. They also underline the fragmentation of the self that occurs during torture, and the subsequent projection of the dissociated parts in the victim's intimate relationships.

Naturally, the inner split will also affect the victim's *self–image* ('I have changed.' 'I am another person now.') The victim cannot anneal the split parts, cannot establish a connection between the person he or she was before and after the traumatic experience. Likewise, the sense of derealization, unreality, creates a general confusion in relation to reality. The boundary between fantasy and reality is changed when reality has proved to be worse than any fantasy imaginable. It later becomes difficult, therefore, to discriminate between the inner and outer world, a state which often leads to paranoid symptoms (ibid).

Lifton (1988, p. 10) emphasizes that dissociation interrupts and distorts the symbolizing process: 'The mind needs the nourishment provided by the continuous process of creating images and forms in order to function well'. Distortion of the symbolizing process is described by Weinstein and Lira (1987, p. 56) as a formation of new symbols through which the outer world, the body, feelings and words take on new meanings associated with the abuse.

During sexual abuse a certain power relationship is established between perpetrator and victim in which the dignity of the victim is attacked – she or he is placed in an inferior position. Afterwards, this inferior role may be re-enacted, consciously or unconsciously, in the victim's relationship to her/his self and in the relationship to significant others: family members, or for example, ethnic or political group. This process of *victimization* is associated with the victim's reactions during the abuse, especially if she has been forced to betray her loved ones or her ideals. Victimization could also be described as a 'moral trauma', because it violates the person's feelings of dignity and moral integrity.

Thus, the abuse is an assault on three of the most fundamental prerequisites for what we could call 'basic trust': the world is benevolent; life has meaning; I have worth. Jerome D. Frank (1973) characterizes the effects of such a shattering experience by the term 'demoralization', in which he tries to summarize the essence of much psychic suffering. I consider this concept particularly characteristic of the feelings of complicity, shame, contamination and loss of self-respect which are often contained in the suffering of those subjected to sexual assault. Such a demoralizing experience can even shake the foundation of our cultural system of meaning. Anthropologist Clifford Geertz does not speak of basic trust, but of *patterns of meaning, symbol and conception*, and he defines culture as:

> a historically transmitted pattern of meanings embodied in symbols, a system of inherited conceptions expressed in symbolic forms by means of which men communicate, perpetuate, and develop their knowledge about and attitudes towards life. (Geertz 1973, p. 89)

The state of demoralization can therefore also be described as a state of '*being outside of culture*'.

When our fundamental assumptions about the world or our historically transferred patterns of meaning are shaken, serious anxiety is created. But if we succeed in giving a new meaning to chaos and cleanse ourselves of shame and impurity, then this can also be the beginning of a revision of the traditional patterns of meaning. In this way, a traumatic experience can also become a transforming experience of great positive value. The stories from The Blue Room attempt, in both form and content, to retain both sides of this process: the traumatic and the liberating; the ugly and the beautiful; the evil and the good.

Form and process of the meeting

'I remember everything in relation to my pregnancies, births and children', Ana says. We are sitting in The Blue Room, and I have just started the tape recorder. All I know about Ana is that she is a political refugee from a certain country in Latin America.

We look at each other, and I try to sense where I can find a connection between us. How can I, together with Ana, create a feeling of fellowship in this room that can be felt directly as having a healing effect around us and between us? The tape recorder stands there as a possible symbol of this fellowship; it can register our words, and in that way they can perhaps acquire a power that reaches beyond the here-and-now. But first we must symbolically invite this fellowship. Therefore, I ask Ana to say her name and her country into the microphone; then we rewind the tape and hear her voice in the room.

Ana has heard her name and her voice. We are ready to start her story.

For me this is also a confrontation with myself: do I have the intuition and courage to accompany Ana on the voyage to the past and lead her further when she hesitates? Does she have the will and courage to call forth a story that is so disturbing that it almost cannot be told?

In this room, our meeting place, we can perhaps establish this third culture which belongs neither to the one nor the other, but develops in the space inside the therapeutic room, but also outside, in field work for example. Here, the ethnographer always sees him or herself at the same time as seeing the others. Cultures are constituted in their implicit contrast to one another, and the others are understood as 'other' in relation to one's self (Hastrup 1986). In this meeting between two cultures (and are not all meetings between people a meeting between two worlds?) I have consciously sought what is common among women, well aware that local variations exist. Instead of making the cultural differences the problem and the object of my investigation, I have followed Geertz when he warns against both cultural universalism and cultural relativism. In the long conflict in anthropology between these two schools, the cultural universalists have emphasized the basic similarities between cultures worldwide, while the cultural relativists have stressed the untranslatable differences between cultures. Perhaps we should rather see ourselves among 'the others' as a local example of a form of human life – one example among many of what it is to be a human being. To see 'the others' as human beings is the least we can do, Geertz remarks (1983). So in this meeting I have tried to create a meeting point in the common third to which we each contribute with our likenesses and differences.

In The Blue Room, I meet 40 'local examples' of women in exile: women from ten different countries: six Middle Eastern (Iran, Iraq, Turkey, Lebanon, Israel and Jordan) and four Latin American (Chile, Argentina, Uruguay and El Salvador). In the Middle Eastern group, six different ethnic groups are represented. Since refugee circles are so small in Denmark, I have chosen for reasons of anonymity to use the imprecise identification: 'Middle Eastern' or 'Latin American'. I chose to meet refugee women from these two groups, because that enabled me to contact a group of women (Latin American) who have been in Denmark for many years and a group of more recent refugees from the Middle East. The Latin American women have lived in Denmark for about twelve years, while those from the Middle East have been here an average of four years (ranging from four months to 21 years).

The Middle Eastern women, most of whom are still in the crisis of the arrival phase, tell of their meeting with the country of exile as it feels when you arrive. And, detail how it is to be a woman rebel in a predominantly androcentric culture. The Latin American women speak of their children and marriages in the long period of exile. For them, so long has elapsed since the traumatic experiences in their homelands, that the distance in time – and the psychological distance – enables them to speak of their traumas with some degree of equanimity.

This is not a comparative study of the two groups, but rather I let the Latin American and Middle Eastern stories supplement each other and provide nuances to the whole narrative – *one testimony* from women in exile.

Before meeting, each woman had received a letter explaining the aim and theme of the study, and a description of my earlier work; they are therefore attuned to my idea. At the beginning of the meeting, I explain the testimony method, stress my position as 'non-neutral' researcher and psychologist, and speak of my earlier work with traumatized refugees, emphasizing the importance of developing new knowledge, especially about refugee women's lives and conditions. I try right from the beginning to communicate a feeling of women's solidarity toward the abuse to which they have been subjected.

The meetings usually last on average around three hours – some twice as long, some shorter. I try to concentrate the testimony on two main themes: how the individual woman has become a refugee; and her life in the homeland and in exile. In this way I attempt to capture both the political and the private aspects of her story. I always begin by asking the woman about how she came to be a refugee in Denmark today. In response she starts to tell her political story. No written questions are used during this phase; the aim is to obtain as complete a story as the woman wishes to tell about her political engagement (if such is the case), the forms of persecution she has been subjected to, her flight and later arrival to exile in Denmark. This usually takes about half of our time together. In some cases, for reasons of security, the woman does not wish to relate any details about the political groups in which she has been active; of course, I respect this wish. Telling the political story usually creates strong contact and a good transition to telling the private story.

For this part of the dialogue, I use a guideline, 'Suggested topics for consciousness-raising', which was developed by New York Radical Feminists during the culmination of the women's movement toward the end of the 1960s (undated, mimeo., distributed in Denmark). Based on the testimony method, it includes detailed questions about sexual development, sexual trauma, marriage, housework, pregnancies, births, motherhood, divorce, work, and age. These questions always relate to the woman's *interpretation* of her situation, that is, not so much hard facts but rather the connection between the private experiences and the social conditions.

As a basis for interviews with these marginalized refugee women it is more appropriate than professional sexological or psychological questionnaires, which would be unable to capture nearly so well the ideological aspects of a refugee woman's consciousness. Asking questions based on a Western feminist consciousness often results in surprising answers. I make a 'trans-cultural juxtaposition' – that is, an equal parallel between two cultures (Marcus & Fischer 1986). This trans-cultural parallel between Western feminist ideology and 'refugee woman's ideology' means that questions are asked from the common ground shared by the marginal position of both a critical Western–woman consciousness and a political–refugee woman consciousness. At the same time, the historical and cultural differences produce new and unexpected perspectives.

Most surprising for me is the women's openness with respect to sexual subjects. This provokes me to question some of my own prejudices about women from foreign cultures and also the so-called 'free' sexuality of the West – a subject that women from the Middle East especially are eager to debate with me.

The point of departure of non-neutral solidarity is fruitful for building up the 'common third'. The risk exists, however, for mutual 'seduction' in a kind of empathetic relationship. Both parties can come to 'idealize' each other and thus avoid uncomfortable subjects or feelings out of fear of destroying this ideal picture – both of oneself and the other person. It can be difficult to sense differences and disagreements, and to ask difficult questions. Sometimes, I choose to stop if I sense that the woman (or I, myself) cannot bear to go further; at others, I meet the woman later to work further therapeutically with the material from the first meeting. All the women agree that their stories are to be published in anonymous form. As underlined earlier, publication of the story of human rights violations is also a guiding thought behind the idea of testimony. The events must be denounced and documented before any healing process can begin.

The women participants

The Latin American women who have lived in Denmark for many years speak fluent Danish; of the Middle Eastern women, who have been here a much shorter time, 16 speak either Danish or English; an interpreter was therefore used in four cases. In transcribing the testimonies, grammatical corrections were essential, but of course, the meaning has been retained.

Three of the women are previous clients; one has assisted me as interpreter, and one I had contacted through solidarity work. These five women have served as my contacts to the refugee circles, and through them I gained access to the other women. There can be significant problems in connection with finding women among Middle Eastern refugees who dare to tell their stories openly. It was therefore of inestimable value that relationships of trust had already been established between me and some of the women through my previous therapeutic work. Among refugees from the Middle East, there is – with good reason – much anxiety about revealing both political and private information. Their circles are infiltrated, and family members in the homeland are commonly persecuted because of those in exile. For this reason, too, I use the term 'Middle Eastern' for the whole group, especially so that women from Iran and Iraq cannot be identified.

In a statistical sense, the group I have chosen to meet is thus 'non-random'. It is probably distinctive in relation to the norm (but no one knows the 'norm', since there is no comprehensive statistical study of refugee women); it is probably distinguished by the level of education, political consciousness and attitude to religion. Most of the group are well-educated: over half either have a university degree or were studying at the time of flight; most were politically active; about half had rejected their religion. They are to a large degree 'dangerous' women who have been (or could be) active fighters in the forefront of the struggle to improve conditions for their less privileged sisters at home.

I choose to meet this group of refugee women, because then I have an optimal opportunity to clarify the subject of my investigation. This marginal group – like others – has a special observation post in the borderland, and a keen consciousness about life on both sides of the border: a position which enables them to speak of control and discipline with nuances and insight. Characteristically, the women in The Blue Room have a strong personal and political motivation to tell their stories. Thus, an intense contact is created and a narrative evolves that is also intense and powerful. The spectrum of traumatic experiences to which such an elite group of refugee women has been subjected is impressive telling; the repression of such 'dangerous' women is severe. Almost all the women have been exposed to one or more forms of political violence: 20 had to live illegally for a long period; 16 experienced serious threats; seven were imprisoned and tortured; five experienced the murder or 'disappearance' of their partners; four experienced severe war traumas; and two had to leave behind small children when they went into exile.

The researcher/therapist: relationship to participants

From the many hours of talking together and the wealth of information I received in The Blue Room, this narrative has evolved. It is my narrative in the sense that through my presence in the room, I influence what is told. I am present, as woman, therapist, researcher and witness; the choice of voices is influenced by my personal, professional and ideological background. I also choose the theoretical sources used in the reframing of the stories. This narrative is therefore created in the meeting between the researcher and the others, each with their story and their qualities.

But what happens to the field worker or therapist in her meeting with the suffering? What kind of *transference* or *counter-transference reactions* are triggered by this meeting with sexual and political violence? A challenging meeting between two people affects them both (Agger & Jensen in press). Just as the anthropologist in a meeting with another culture is unavoidably affected and must therefore also be 'her own informant' (Hastrup 1986), the therapist's registration of her own counter-transference is also an important source of information about the world of the victim. Field workers, like therapists, must be able to confront that which is foreign and perhaps frightening without defending themselves inappropriately. Otherwise, it will be difficult for them to experience what is going on in the field around them. In The Blue Room, the field worker is also a psychologist with clinical experience, and this provides the possibility to relate consciously to the transference relationship contained in the situation in which difficult stories full of conflict are told. At the same time, this background also contains the possibility of meeting the strong and liberating aspects of the stories.

The confrontation with violence demands a defence of some kind, but the researcher (and therapist) must try to be conscious of how she or he protects herself, must try to maintain boundaries so that she or he is experienced as safe and secure; but these boundaries must not be so rigid that the researcher is experienced as cold and distant. At the same time, in efforts to be warm and engaged, she must avoid losing herself or drowning in the feelings that necessarily arise in a meeting with a traumatic story.

The researcher/therapist therefore also needs a place where she or he can tell the story about the meeting. In other words, a forum to express the difficult and conflict-ridden story and gain insight as to how to protect oneself. In my case, perhaps to write down the narrative from The Blue Room. In the confrontation with violence and assault, we meet universal, existential questions which Geertz (1973, pp. 87–141) calls 'the problem of evil', 'the problem of suffering' – in the final sense, 'the problem about meaning'. It is not a coincidence that researchers (and therapists) who work within this area often end their presentations of the problem by raising existential questions. This is also the case for the direct victims of violence: the meaningless suffering and evil are unbearable. Everyone seeks meaning, understanding, a larger context.

With this map of the territory, we will now begin the voyage towards the past.

2. The Daughter's Room

In this space, the girl began to sense the meaning of being a woman in an androcentric culture. Here, she discovered the social and cultural significance of the physical changes occurring in her body. Inside this space, she moved through the various states marked by her transition from girl to virgin to woman, and discovered and defined the meaning of being a woman in a male-centred universe.

The narrative of The Daughter's Room is based on the stories of the Middle Eastern women, who in an especially radical way voiced experiences also found in other androcentric societies. Although some of what they relate can seem foreign to us in the context of Western culture, it is not so strange and different that we do not recognize elements in this narrative. These stories will naturally have local variations, both in relation to the individual girl and to the cultural space in which The Daughter's Room belongs. Thus, this is not a 'universal' or unambiguous narrative of growing up as a girl. But we find in these Middle Eastern stories some elements, which in the context of knowledge about women's situation in other cultures, do provide a kind of 'syndrome' (Ardener 1987) which finds expression in different ways and with different power with various androcentric cultures.

In the Middle Eastern women's rebellion against a structure which distinctly defines them in relation to their value as objects for men, we recognize a woman's story about dilemma and ambivalence: on the one hand, the desire to be free and to define oneself; on the other hand, the desire to live in the safety of a protective system. To rebel against such deeply rooted social and cultural mores means rupture, loss and anxiety, but also self-awareness, pride and self-respect.

We can illustrate this ambiguity through the relationship to *blood*. In this narrative, blood has great symbolic significance because it is the outward sign of the transition from one stage to another. The first menstruation marks the transition from girl to virgin, while the blood of defloration marks the transition from virgin to woman. But because blood symbolizes these important transitions, a whole world of contradictory social and emotional associations is connected to it. Blood symbolizes something beautiful and pure, and simultaneously something dangerous, unclean and shameful.

On the symbolic level, blood, according to anthropologist Mary Douglas (1966), is one of the *marginal* substances. Marginality here refers to our inner picture of society. This picture has form: it has outer boundaries, marginal areas and an internal structure. The marginal area is dangerous, because if it is pulled too far in one direction or another, it threatens the system's boundaries. The orifices of the body symbolize its most vulnerable points, and thereby represent threatened or sensitive boundaries – both bodily and social. Douglas sees all the substances emitted through the body's openings as belonging to this marginal and dangerous area. This is symbolized by the risk of pollution and contamination that is connected with them. There are variations from one culture to another as to which powers are invested in the bodily substances, depending on which social structure the body mirrors. Douglas thus sees the relationship to the body as a symbol of relations in the surrounding society. The power and danger found within the social structure are reproduced in the symbolism of the body.

In this narrative of The Daughter's Room, the relationship to blood reflects the woman's position in an androcentric culture. Its appearing – or even more important its failure to appear – is a decisive signal regarding status, social boundaries which are crossed, and perhaps social boundaries which have been violated. There is no doubt about the dangerous power of blood in this narrative.

The girl's blood

The first bleeding? I didn't like it. I put on something tight around my breasts so no one could see that I had grown up. In our society, it is better to stay a little girl. When you begin to grow up, attitudes change so much. But when I got my first bleeding, I went to my mother and told her, because – she is really a wonderful woman, and I can tell her everything. But I saw what happened in other families. My girlfriends were so afraid to speak of these things. But I went to my mother and said: 'I have a sore'. I did not know what it was. Of course, I had heard something from my sisters. I have three older sisters, and they talked about things I didn't understand but that I thought about. They said, for example: "I am not clean. I cannot do this or that. I am not clean; I'm bleeding." I didn't know what these words meant, and I didn't ask. Maybe because I had such a feeling of self-respect and my family looked on me as such a perfect person I wanted to preserve that beautiful picture.

But I asked my mother about it, and she said: "It is good. Now, you have become a lovely woman and that is very good." I remember she worried more about my health than before, and gave me many things to eat, saying: "This is good for you while you are growing." In my country, they think so much about this bleeding. Because if a girl doesn't bleed, she can't become a mother. And that is what is important. Because if a woman doesn't get pregnant, she can expect a very bad future. She will be a nobody, because she cannot work or support herself. That is why my mother was so happy when I told her. Then she knew that I was a normal girl. Later, when I was grown up and travelled to many other places and met other women and other kinds of families, I heard what they said about women who couldn't be pregnant. But I didn't know then why my mother was so happy. (Middle East)

Until the girl crosses the threshold that changes attitudes to such a degree, she has the freedom to define herself. From then on, however, she enters a space with another significance; one which is defined by her reproductive function. The girl's first blood represents the beautiful, pure picture of motherhood, supported by the girl's own mother – but it is also unclean, as she learns from her older sisters. She has sensed already as a little girl, through the women's fellowship, that blood came from a vulnerable and dangerous area.

It was very difficult when I began to develop into a woman. I got my menstruation when I was eleven, and I was very embarrassed about my breasts. I always walked on the street with round shoulders so they wouldn't see my breasts. When I got my menstruation the first time, I was very shy. What should I say to my mother? It was a great crisis in my life, because now I could no longer go out in the street or play with the boys, and they kept saying that now I could not play with the small children, now that I had become a woman. For them, it meant that one was a woman, not an eleven-year-old girl.

I talked about it first with my oldest sister. I cried and asked what I should do. Because for us it was all secret, how a woman got her menstruation, what she should do, why her stomach hurt. Therefore, it was a shock for me: what was it? There was some blood, and I didn't know what it was. I had not heard anything about it. Now, I teach my daughter all about these things, but with us, the mother did not explain to the girls. We grow up, and we find out for ourselves.

So I went in to my sister and told her, and it made her happy and she said: "Now, you are grown up – you are no longer a little girl. It will come every month, and you must take care of yourself and eat well when you have it. And you should do thus and so." She simply taught me what to do. I first told my mother two years later. I was too shy to tell her. But she said that I should not be shy, that it was normal for girls to get it.

But they teased us about being grown up. For example, my aunt said: "What are you doing? You are a big girl now!" I was afraid they would tease me, so I didn't want to tell anyone. But my sister didn't tease me. She helped me buy everything I needed. But after that, my whole life changed. I always had to be careful, careful. (Middle East)

One must *be careful*, otherwise one can disturb the order of things. 'The ideal order of society is guarded by dangers which threaten transgressors' (Douglas 1966, p. 3). One of the serious dangers that threaten those who are not careful is contamination or *impurity*. Dirt is defined by Douglas as 'something' which is in the wrong place. The unclean and the dirty must not be present if the structure is to be maintained. If you disturb the order of things by transgressing certain boundaries you expose yourself to dangerous pollution.

But you not only pollute yourself. You are also dangerous for others. You become a potential source of contagion. And, as Douglas observes, the polluting person's intentions are completely irrelevant. The danger of pollution is a power that threatens careless people against whom the structure is expected to protect itself: 'A polluting person is always in the wrong. He has developed some wrong condition or simply crossed some line which should not have been crossed and this displacement unleashes danger for someone' (Ibid. p. 113). Therefore, it is a relief if the others can help you to be careful, otherwise it can be difficult to know when you are being careless:

When we are little girls, our families never repress us. We are allowed to play outside and everything. But it begins when we grow up. Then, we have to be careful, and we like it, too. We don't wish to be free. But nobody told me about menstruation, and when I saw the blood the first time, I started to cry. I remember I ran to my mother and said that something awful had happened, that some blood had come. And she said: "You mustn't be afraid of that, you mustn't be afraid. That is a fine thing." And she began to teach me. She said: "Now, you are grown up. Now, you are a woman." But she hadn't told me before. With my own daughters, I told them about it when they were eight–ten years old. I didn't want them to go through the same experience.

But you know, I had heard about it through my religion and from my cousins. We were a large family, and I listened to them when they talked together. And I also saw things. As a little girl I knew about it [menstruation] but my mother never told me about it. I didn't know it would also happen to me. I thought that maybe the others had something that was special. So I was frightened and I cried, and my mother said that it was all right. But that was a long time ago. Now, it is different for girls in my country. (Middle East)

Something mysterious and secret is also connected to the dangerous and forbidden. But even so, bits of information can be gathered within the women's fellowship, and there is resistance to the boundaries which are formed around the woman's body in an androcentric culture:

It was a surprise when my body began to develop. Because as you know women wore veils in my country when I was a child, and I felt that they were ashamed of their woman's body. Maybe that is why I was ashamed of my own body when I grew up. From the time I was 14 years old – before I was married and had children – I had a nice body then. I was proud of it. And also maybe because my older sister talked to me about it. She told me many things. She told me about menstruation before it came, that it was normal, that it was good. But she is a good woman, not simple-minded. There were many things in our society she didn't care about. (Middle East)

A feeling of *shame* is also connected with acts which are dangerous and impure and which transgress boundaries. The woman's body, as a whole, comes to represent this dangerous area. And one who is careless, or not careful enough with her body, feels shame. We can see shame as the voice of society within the individual, 'the silent speech that founds the social person' (Bidou 1982, p. 141). But in this Daughter's Room, there was also space for rebellion against the power of shame, a refusal to allow this silent voice to form the social being.

I didn't like my body when I began to develop into a woman. I didn't like it. It was different to my sister's. She was very proud of hers. I was a more complicated woman! When I got my first menstruation, I felt that it was something dirty, something unclean – even though I knew that it was completely normal. (Middle East)

The undefinable and contradictory character of a marginal state can become an inner dilemma for one who does not accept her position in the system.

It was very hard for me when I began to develop into a woman because I had always played with boys. I don't know – it was very upsetting to get breasts. I tried to hide them under black clothing. And I didn't say anything about my first menstruation to my mother, either. I had known about it from when I was eight or nine years old because my older sister had told me about it, and my girlfriends in school. We also learned about it in school, in biology. But anyway it was very difficult to accept. I was shy. But finally, I told my mother and she just said: "It's good." And she helped me. It is also a tradition in my country that we don't talk about it very much, even though we learn about it. Irony is used a lot in our culture, and so you are afraid of doing or saying something that the others might laugh at. That limits your possibilities. Maybe you will not be treated in this way, but you wonder what will happen when you become a woman. (Middle East)

It is not possible to know the exact significance of the first blood, but under all circumstances, it constitutes the entrance into a new social existence. It is surrounded by dangers of which you have to be careful, although it is difficult to know precisely of *what* you must be careful. It is a change received as something beautiful, but also as something threatening. The girl's first blood marks the entrance to a special kind of existence. She is neither child nor adult and has therefore no firm social position; she has now entered the state of virginity.

The virginal borderland

The girl now finds herself in a dangerous situation where she is sexually mature, but unmarried. According to Fatima Mernissi (1987), there are two socially acceptable states for a female in the Middle East: the state of the child and the state of the adult, married woman. The situation of the premarital woman is extremely risky, because the menstruating woman is a sexual being who, by being careless, can violate the boundary physically represented by the hymen. Thus, in this world (and in many other androcentric cultures), special dangers are connected with the physical barrier of virginity. A rupture of this barrier equals a social transgression that has almost inconceivable consequences. In some cases, it can endanger life itself:

I thought virgin-worship wrong, but what could I do when everyone thought in this way? And if I were to be married and my husband discovered that I had slept with another man, he would tell my family and they might kill me. I know that has happened in many families. The killers were not the girl's father or brother, but perhaps an uncle or cousin. (Middle East)

Only by protecting her virginity can she maintain her value as an object of exchange for the males in the family. Virginity *is* her honour, or rather, the honour of the male members of her family. The loss of her virginity would signify loss of honour for the whole family – a loss of social status which could be restored only by the family itself. But pity the girl whose hymen is so elastic that there is no bleeding at the first intercourse, or the girl who simply has no hymen. This little membrane is the most important part of her body. According to the Egyptian doctor Nawal el Saadawi (1980) it is worse for a girl to lose her hymen than to lose an eye.

> During the four months we were engaged, I grew to love him so much. At first, I liked him, but during those four months we were together, I came to love him. Therefore, I felt I could sleep with him, but he wouldn't. He said: "I think you should wait until our wedding, because I don't want anyone to speak badly of you or say that you aren't a virgin or anything like that. That would be very bad." He had already slept with others, of course, but he knew his family and mine. He understood the situation much better than I did. Afterwards, I realized it was good that we had waited until our wedding night.
>
> If a girl in my country sleeps with others before she is married, then people call her a whore, a bad girl. I am against this, but it has always been like that in my country, that it is all right for men but not for women. I have had many long discussions with other women from my country here in Denmark. They think, oh, how bad Danish women are because they sleep with men before they are married. But I think that if it is all right for a man, why is it not all right for a woman? OK, for us it is forbidden. In our own country, if a woman sleeps with others before she is married, they say the ugliest things about her – even if it is her betrothed, her future husband. In my country, the men go to whores, not to ordinary girls. All men do that. (Middle East)

Natural, biological phenomena are used everywhere to mark social differences, and virginity is no exception. The cultural significance attached to virginity depends on its position within a larger system of cultural categories. In the Middle East, as well as many other regions of the world, a woman's sexual 'purity' is a symbol of her social purity (Hastrup 1978). A man may, almost must, have sexual relations before marriage. But it would be a threat to the whole family's honour if the woman were polluted in this way. The meeting with Danish culture makes this contradiction clearer and inspires reflection about it. For Western women, virginity does not have the same symbolic value, but we are familiar with expressions such as 'a sweet that has already been sucked', and few women have forgotten how they lost their virginity. It is a special event.

During the five years I was in love with my future husband, he was not allowed to see me. He was only allowed to call me. But he sent secret letters to me – to my girlfriend's house. My family must not learn of it. We also saw each other from a distance, on the street. In fact, he is a relative, and before my family knew that I was in love with him he visited us often. But when they found out, they said: 'Never come to our house again." But we managed to meet sometimes – at night. He called and said: "Meet me at midnight." I slipped out while the whole family slept. We just sat and talked and kissed each other, nothing else. He was also frightened, you know. He was worried about me, for if something came between us, for example if he had a road accident, what would I do? If I should have to marry another and I was not a virgin? Maybe my family would kill me. It is not good for a couple to marry and the girl to be sent back home on the wedding night. Then everybody will know.

But if the girl is not a virgin, the man first asks: "Who is he? Just tell me who he is." And the girl always tells the truth. If she says it was not another man, but that she lost her virginity in another way, he will take her to a doctor. And if the doctor says it is nothing, but only because she has ridden a bike or been active in sports, then he accepts her. But the girl always tells the truth. She will not hurt her husband by letting others look at him and think that he is a fool. This is our way, and I like it. Will you hear the truth? I do not like your life, for sexual freedom is not good. We think about sexuality in a different way from people in the West. We feel that it is holy. It does not only concern a man and a woman. There is something between two people who are married that is very holy. It is not only something I need. Yes, of course, everyone has need of it, but not in the way you do in the West. (Middle East)

Not only in the Middle East but in European Mediterranean cultures too (Hastrup 1978), girls' virginity is used as an object of exchange between males. In a religious sense, virginity is connected with purity. In Christianity, too, Mary's divine power is predicated on her purity.

When this social symbol ceases to function, as is the case for us in Northern Europe, the institution of marriage becomes threatened. In our world, there are other ways of defining women than by their status as mothers and wives. Women are able to support themselves and live as unmarried women, with the social and emotional costs which this freedom also generates. Arrival as a refugee to our country gives a woman the opportunity to see us 'from outside', and at the same time clarify patterns in the life she left behind. It is possible for her to formulate a cultural criticism of the contradictions in our lives, between on the one hand a diffuse freedom to live out impulses, and on the other, the pain she observes to be one of the conditions of this 'free' life.

Before I met my husband, I didn't have a boyfriend. It wasn't because I was against it, but because I thought that I was too young. I should be more grown up and more sure of myself. There were young men who came and talked with me and said that they loved me, but I rejected them. I was not in love with them. So my husband was the first man I loved. I was indifferent to what others thought. Since I loved my husband, I wanted to be with him always. I didn't want to marry him. I just wanted to be together with him. It was a strange thing for a woman to say as I did: "I won't marry you. I will just live together with you." In fact, I told him: "I believe it is bad to marry. It is better just to live together." But he refused. He said: "Are you mad? How can you live with me without being married? You can't do that in our society." Finally, I said: "OK, so we get married." I didn't think it was especially important to be a virgin, but I remained a virgin until we married. I believe it is something I learned both from my family and the society in which I grew up. But it was not only because of my family that I remained a virgin; it was also because I hadn't found a man whom I thought I had to go to bed with. I believe a woman is also a person, that she has the same needs as a man. She also needs to go to bed with a man. And if she doesn't do it, then she is not normal. But my society has also influenced me, for now I have been married for ten years, and sometimes my husband asks me to take the sexual initiative. But I cannot. I do not. Not because I don't want to, but because it is so difficult for me to ask him about it. It is a shameful thing to do. Sometimes I talk to my woman friends about it. Maybe you know el Saadawi? I believe her books are important. She did the same as we do now. (Middle East)

Women can rebel against virgin-worship. The great social significance of virginity actually also gives women *power*. If they refuse to comply, they can destroy the men's game. 'Women are not only objects; they have to agree to behave as objects, too, and if they don't, the men will lose some objects of exchange' (Hastrup 1978, p. 56). But it is difficult to refuse to conform, even with a progressive man, if the whole society is against you. And this form of oppressed female sexuality is so deeply engraved in each woman's consciousness and body, as a cultural and social category, that it is difficult to behave otherwise, even with the knowledge you can acquire from such widely-read books as Nawal el Saadawi's. It is not very different in the West. According to the sexologist Helen Kaplan (1974, p. 350), the belief that women will be rejected if they are sexually active and take the initiative is a part of our cultural heritage. 'Sex is still associated with sin, shame, and/or danger. . . . thus, women who have been taught from an early age to consider passivity and compliance a virtue are likely to react to their impulses to assume a more active role in sex with guilt and shame.'

What is this all about? Boys can do everything. But I couldn't fight against our whole culture and society. Even though I felt differently, I had to live in my country, and if I wanted to marry – whether the man was modern or not – all our men say that girls should be virgins. So I also had to be careful. I knew well that I should keep my virginity, but almost the worst part was the rumours. Once, my sweetheart kissed me on the street and I cried for a week, because I thought that I would get pregnant. I was 17 or 18 before I knew how children are born. My girlfriends and I found a book and read about it. It was customary to find this out two or three days before the wedding. When I began to become politically conscious, I also began to discuss these matters with my friends. In my country, girls must not feel or think about sexuality. Only the man is allowed to do that, and it is he who decides when she can begin to be a sexual being. She must not take the initiative. She may not say no to sexuality either, if she is married. They have murdered our feelings! (Middle East)

Although the events have unfolded in the world of the homeland, the stories are told from exile. That perspective is revealing. The woman sees a conflict between insight and feelings which is so impossible to resolve that the only solution seems to be to repress the troublesome feelings. But this, then, creates new problems in the marriage where she must suddenly become sexually available.

Many of my girlfriends have an unsatisfactory sex life. Many cannot have orgasms. I think that has to do with all the prejudices against sexuality they have grown up with. We must not touch ourselves. Many don't wish to have any sex life, but are forced to it in one way or another. I can't speak openly about sexuality as Danes do. (Middle East)

The notion that Danes – and Western women generally – are so sexually liberated is not confirmed by results of Western sexological research. According to Kaplan (1983), eight per cent of North American women were totally anorgastic; in addition, a very large group had problems having an orgasm. Rather than seeing this as a 'problem of desire', this 'frigidity' can perhaps be understood as resistance to eroticizing repression (Jackson 1987). Refusal to have an orgasm or loss of desire are also powerful weapons against male dominance.

I remember when I was 15, I believed that if a man kissed a girl, she would become pregnant. My mother was pregnant at that time, and I asked her: "Mother, how did you become pregnant? Has father kissed you?" She started to laugh, but didn't explain. I was 17 or 18 before I learned in school about human biology and found out how you become pregnant. I couldn't ask my older sister, because it was also a secret. They must not tell me. Not until a girl is married is she allowed to ask her mother about it and get an explanation. I remember that after my sister was married I asked her: "What has he done to you?" And she answered: "You'll find out for yourself when you marry." They are not allowed to explain. And if women sit and talk about pregnancy or menstruation, they tell the unmarried girls: "Go outside!" We must not hear what they say. They are afraid that maybe we will do something wrong if we hear about it before we are married, that we will lose our virginity. (Middle East)

Knowledge is considered dangerous. For knowledge gives power. As long as something is secret, it is easier to maintain control. To the secret is attached something exciting but also something dangerous which is difficult to define and thus induces a sense of having to be constantly careful not to commit forbidden acts.

Virginity is the most important thing, for the most educated people too. They are so worried about it. I don't think that way, but in my society even educated and intelligent men do – really, even though they may say something else. While I was at the university, I didn't believe in this virginity business, but I didn't meet anyone with whom I was in love and would have given it to. It was the books I read that changed my view of virginity so that it no longer meant anything to me. The translated books we read are the first and most important sources for changing our consciousness. (Middle East)

When it is no longer secret, the closed structure is opened towards influences from the outside. It is an opening which makes it difficult for those in power to maintain control. In the next story, however, we learn from a woman who is still a virgin how difficult it is to free oneself of the sense of danger associated with the body's boundaries. Her strong psychic attitude toward the body remains intact despite the fact that her sexual political consciousness tells her something else:

Virginity meant a lot to me. Even though I had never spoken to my mother about it, nor had she ever said to me: "You must do this and that because you are a girl, in order not to lose your virginity." My parents never said that. But I heard about it at school or from my friends, of course, and they also spoke about it at home, even though it wasn't a big problem. But at school, for example, we heard about a girl who was together with a boy and became pregnant, and how sad it was for her and how she became isolated and expelled from school.

My attitude today is that in biological terms, virginity has no meaning for me. I feel it doesn't matter whether a girl is a virgin or not. But the attitude in the Muslim world, is a religious view, and when you are raised in a Muslim society, then you develop a strong psychic attitude toward it. You *must* be a virgin until you are married, and you don't learn very much about other people elsewhere in the world where it is quite normal not to be a virgin. They tell us that if one is a virgin and makes some mistake, God will forgive us, because one is pure. In the Koran it says that if virgins make mistakes in their lives, God will forgive them. If a woman goes to bed with a man, she is considered a bad woman. She is unclean and is isolated by the others: "We must not talk to her because she is a bad woman. She is not good; we will have nothing to do with her because she can influence others." It is a religious sin. Therefore, there are various things one must avoid doing. For example, one must not ride a bike, jump, participate in sports like volleyball. This promotes a passive personality in women. In this way, you are raised to be passive. This happens regardless of the political repression. It is a cultural or psychological development that represses the will to be active. It is forbidden to speak of your sexual needs. You must simply not speak of it.

Of course, girls talk about it to each other. One girl is in love, for example, and what should she do? She will not marry, so what should she do? You may be in love only at a distance. You must not touch. But the girl comes in contact with the one she loves, secretly. Maybe on the way to school, they speak to each other, or maybe they go to the movies; that is the only way.

In our political party, we do not view it as a sin if a girl loses her virginity, but personally I think I still believe in this virgin ideology. I am very conscious about it. With my political consciousness, I reject it. There are many girls like me who reject it. They don't think it important to be a virgin and go by religious rules. We feel it is very important to discuss these things within the political group, and we read various ideological opinions. But in our view the family is extremely important. In my opinion it is acceptable for a girl to live with a boy without being married. Many women refugees from my country already do that. But in our own country, you must be very careful because we live in a very religious society with another ideology and another way of thinking. We must be very aware of other people's view of these things. Because even though we believe that people are free to choose how they will live, when we live among religious people, we must not provoke them. For example, two members of my party living in my homeland married, even though they didn't feel it was necessary for their own sakes. We believe it is enough if two people agree and accept one another as their partner; but the society cannot accept it. We need some kind of evidence that we are married, and in my country this cannot be provided at the city hall. It must be given through a religious ceremony. But that does not mean that we ourselves are religious.

It is very difficult for me, however, to surrender my virginity outside marriage. I cannot accept a sexual relationship with a man without being married, even though there is no one who watches over me. No one controls me now. There is no one to say anything to me about it.

I experienced a real problem when I had to visit a Danish gynaecologist. In my country, a gynaecological examination of a virgin is done anally, but not here. I once went to the emergency ward of a Copenhagen hospital because I had terrible pain in my lower abdomen. A woman gynaecologist attended me and she said she had to examine me to see why I had this pain. I said to her: "You must be careful. I am a virgin and wish to remain one." She answered: "That's OK. Just lie down." And then she began to put a long rod in me. I said: "No, you must not do that." "Why not?" she asked. I said: "But I told you. I am a virgin. I don't want to lose it." "It is all right. I will only examine you," she replied, and then she said something I didn't understand and continued to examine me. So I screamed: "No, I will not be examined. I told you that I don't want to be examined in this way." I thought there were other ways to be examined. I was afraid of all those instruments. I couldn't stand it and began to cry. The gynaecologist asked: "What is the matter?" She thought I cried because I was pregnant. The nurses stood and talked about it. I could hear them say: "She is afraid." They said: "Just tell us. What is the matter? Do you have any problems?" I answered: "I don't have any problems with my sex life. I just don't like those long rods, and I told you that since I am a virgin, you must take care." Finally, the gynaecologist said: "I can't examine you. You need to be examined with ultra-sound and that is very expensive. We don't do that here." So I said: "OK, then I won't be examined. Goodbye."

The next day I went to my own doctor who referred me to a private gynaecologist who was very kind. Mostly, I just talked to her about my problems. She explained how she could examine me without damaging my virginity. And it worked out fine. (Middle East)

This is both a story about different cultural categories and about different degrees of sensitivity on the part of the gynaecologists. Since there was never any *meeting* between the woman and the first gynaecologist, a working alliance was never created between them. The story of the consultation with the second gynaecologist shows that such a meeting was possible. Apparently she knew that pain can have causes other than purely physical ones. Maybe the first gynaecologist would use the concept of 'cultural differences' to explain the problems in the contact between herself and the patient from a foreign culture. This would be an easy explanation which freed her from the responsibility of meeting her patient as a human being rather than only as a body. It would also be a simplified explanation. Each person's interpretation of their cultural categories is different and often contradictory, as we have seen, and the 'alien' cultural categories are not all so strange and different after all.

> I had often thought about how it [sexual intercourse] would be the first time, whether it would hurt, or whether I would come to the hospital. But I think it was very normal for me. Of course, it was something different because I had never tried it before, and unlike Danish girls, I wasn't 14 or 15, I was 25 then. It was while I was in transit, waiting to come to Denmark. If I had done it in my own country, I would perhaps never have married, because it is very difficult for girls who are not virgins; most men want a wife who is a virgin. I told my mother, she was a little angry at first, but then she said: "Now you live alone. When you live in another country I cannot decide how you shall live or what you shall do."
>
> My boyfriend now is also a refugee from my country. He doesn't think it important whether or not I am a virgin. The important thing is whether we love each other. When you have lived outside my country for two or three years, you forget certain things or choose to act differently. In my country, you can find men who will marry a girl who isn't a virgin; they will say: "I love this girl. It doesn't matter what she has done before."
>
> But sometimes I'm worried about the future because I'm not married. What will happen in a few years? What if I get sick? But I can't just go out on the street and find a man who will marry me. (Middle East)

She has violated the commandment, and although she is now living in a country where this is accepted, and it is more or less acceptable to her mother and lover, she is still a little uncomfortable about it. The lover from her homeland has not married her, although he claims that virginity means nothing to him. It is a very decisive boundary which is symbolized by the next blood: the blood that marks the transition from the virginal borderland to the important social role of the married woman.

The man's blood

The virgin state can be seen as a kind of 'third sex', preceding the state of the woman, the 'second sex'. It is through a man, however, that a virgin becomes a woman. The man thus destroys the virgin's purity, but at the same time transforms her into a pure woman (Hastrup 1978), if, indeed, the sign of the second bleeding is on the sheet on the wedding night.

I was very afraid of the first night, and there were two nights before that. . . . The first time was disturbing because we waited to see whether there was blood. For a woman, that means a great deal – and for me, too, it meant a great deal. I waited to see whether I was a real girl or not, even though I knew I was. But does the blood come or not? That proves whether or not it is the first time. The first night is not fun, because you are afraid. I was, and many of my friends said they were – afraid as to whether they were real girls.

In many families, it is still the custom to show the blood [stained sheet] to the mother-in-law, to the women in the husband's family so they cannot talk afterward. But we didn't do that. After the first time, I asked him: "Is it necessary to show it to your mother?" And he said: "No, how silly you are. It is I who am the most important, not my mother or the others. If you show them, then they might interfere with your life later." So I didn't do it.

At first, I wouldn't show my feelings when we were in bed together. But later, I sensed that my husband thought it strange that I didn't talk and didn't say that I thought it was nice. Then I understood that now I had that opportunity, and could show how I felt. I didn't know him very well. I didn't know whether he would think I was a bad girl. Only after a couple of years did I dare begin to tell him how nice it was, before then I didn't know how he would react.

This was something that went back to my childhood, when I gradually came to understand what sex was. I understood from the women around me that one should pretend to be sexually innocent; to act as if one knew nothing about sex and had no experience. That is what I did, because I thought I should. Once, I read that our Prophet Mohammed had said that during the day a woman should be sweet, pure and innocent, but at night a whore for her husband. What does that mean? She should show her feelings and may do all kinds of things to attract her husband when they are together at night. But during the day, before others, she must act like a pure, innocent woman. I thought then: "That can't be right. One should be the same day and night, and act as if one knew nothing about sex, with one's husband too." But later, I understood that Mohammed was right. Before other men, and women, while a woman must be natural and talk with them, within certain limits, at night, alone with her husband, there must be no limits.

To show the wedding-night blood to the women of her husband's family is to acknowledge their power. If she maintains her ambiguity – is she pure or impure – they are forced to be more cautious. But the most important person, her husband, must know that she is pure. And although she must suddenly behave like an impure woman, that conflict can be solved; she learns that it is possible to be both pure and impure at the same time. The ambiguity she thus acquires in the relationship to her husband as well also gives her a certain power, forcing caution on him too.

My husband comes from a family full of the old ideas. It is their custom for an old woman of the family to be present the first night, to ensure that the girl is really a virgin. During the first two weeks of our marriage, I fought with this old woman without uttering a word. I decided I wouldn't do it [sexual intercourse] while she was there; my husband agreed. He was very sweet, he didn't get angry, perhaps he didn't want to do it while she was there, either. People with new ideas turn against those things they had earlier. When my sister came to visit us, the old woman said to her: "Why hasn't your sister done it? It is very important." My sister laughed at her, and then the woman left the house. (Middle East)

Rebellion against ancient traditions becomes a silent and stubborn struggle between the old and young woman. And this silent struggle also frees the husband from having to produce the important blood on the sheet. He may be just as anxious about the performance as she is; both are parts of a structure they have not chosen. New ideas give you possibilities of acting differently – you might even make fun of what in earlier times could have been extremely dangerous.

The night before my wedding, I sat with a group of women from my family and they talked and joked about it [sex]. They were happy and said that there was nothing to be afraid of; I should just relax. "You will be happy afterwards. You will enjoy it," they said. And they prepared everything for the wedding. They sewed a special kind of white towel which the bride uses to dry herself. It was very fine, and my mother was very proud of me, her daughter. She wanted to keep that towel afterwards, because the whole family would ask her about it. But everything was not so nice when I said that I didn't want anyone to see that towel. My mother said: "You must decide for yourself." But I wanted to make my mother happy. Why not? So two or three months later, I gave it to her, but not the same night. Mothers ask even though they know it's not especially nice. But I didn't want her to be unhappy. Why shouldn't she have the pleasure of being proud of me?

I am still in love with my husband. I think no woman loves her husband as I do. I worry about him. I am sad when he is sad. I don't want any evil to come to him, ever, ever. I love him much more now than at first. He is the best in my life. He makes me feel strong, and I make him feel strong. We think in the same way.

But after that first night, I cried because I was not used to these things. I was only 18. But afterwards, I was completely crazy about him. I enjoyed it. I was very happy. When he was away, I was crazy, because I missed him so. (Middle East)

She struggles against the old tradition, but at last chooses to give in. Rebellion would be costly not only for herself, but also for her mother. By failing to show her mother the sign of her virginity, she could shame her. Instead she must take the shame on herself by displaying her blood. The wedding night is both an extremely private and extremely public event. It can be difficult to solve this conflict for oneself:

On my wedding night, after three or four hours, then – I don't know whether it was because my husband wanted to show it [the blood stain] to them – but we came out to drink tea; they were still celebrating. I didn't want all that about showing them the cloth, but later my mother came to fetch it, otherwise the man's family can say all kinds of things. It is good for me and my family that they see my blood, because what if they say bad things about me? They start to say things about many women who get married, that something happened . . . they can say evil things about her. (Middle East)

No wonder the first night can be so traumatic that it causes sexual problems. The woman in the next account experienced severe pain during intercourse. That condition may have physical causes, for example infection; it often occurs when the woman is not sufficiently aroused before intercourse, or if she is treated brutally or sadistically (Kaplan 1983). Whether she is abnormal or 'frigid' is difficult to determine because of the secrecy which surrounds everything sexual:

I was very frightened the first time I went to bed with my husband. I was also afraid of becoming pregnant, but my husband explained that to me. Men have good opportunities to read about sexuality, but not women. If I go to a book store to buy such a book, and a man sees me, for example the salesman, that would mean that I am a bad woman. I had read one book about women and sexuality, about women and how they are oppressed by society; it was by Nawal el Saadawi. When I bought it, I was afraid and put a paper cover on it. But my father opened it anyway and asked: "What is it called, *Women and Sexuality*?" And I said: "It's a good book. You can read it, for it is not about sex. It is more about society's oppression of girls and about how they think."

But the first time was a shock, and afterwards I thought I was sexually cold, because I felt no desire. But maybe it was because I couldn't love him. There were bad feelings between us, and it got worse after a year. I had absolutely no desire to go to bed with him, but he forced me to do it, and he wanted it every day. I felt so badly, because a woman must not say no, and many times, when I said no anyway, the next day was awful. He quarrelled with me all the time and ordered me to do the marketing and cook even though we both studied at the university.

It really hurt when I made love with him, because I was too small, and I didn't understand why that was. After four years, I spoke to my sister about it; she lived in England. She said: "Why do you have pain? Women don't usually experience pain when they go to bed with their husbands." I told her that I had pain every time, and that I couldn't walk so well the day after. She said that meant that I didn't have the right feelings for him, and that I couldn't live with him any longer. She also wondered why I didn't say no if I had no desire to make love. The problem was that everything about sex is very secret. Therefore, I couldn't say anything to anyone, or ask any of my friends or my sisters about it. I thought that I wasn't normal, that I was cold because I had no desire. Maybe there was something wrong with my body. But after talking to my sister, I discovered that our whole relationship was wrong. (Middle East)

It is difficult to break out of a relationship even though it feels all wrong. Divorce is a decisive break with cultural and social categories. In exile, the conflict is sharpened because the woman finds herself in a cultural context where divorce is both economically possible and acceptable:

The women I know, myself included, know exactly what is supposed to happen the first night. And we don't like it, just because we know about it. We have a bad picture of it. We feel it just like a knife that cuts. I got my husband to play chess the first night, in order to postpone it. One or two months would be fine. But he calmed me down. But others, I am sure cry afterwards. The first night is a terrible night for our women.

I said to my husband: "Be kind and don't do it. Let us just be friends." And to test him I told him that I was not a virgin. He only answered that he didn't mind. In our society it is very strange for a girl to say that she has lost her virginity, that she has done it before. No matter how close you are as a couple, the man cannot accept it. But I said it just to test him as a person, and I made him believe it. He answered that me as a person was important to him, not what had happened to me. That was the good thing about him, but it is not easy to speak about these things.

We didn't do it the first night, but the second when I felt I had control of the situation: he would do it when *I* was ready. That made me feel better. We could decide together. But others cannot say "Be sweet and don't do it." Then, the man would think that there was something wrong with the woman, that she wasn't a virgin. Some keep their eyes closed, or take on a blindfold.

After the first night, though, I understood many things I hadn't understood before. The most important was that I really loved my husband. But a week later, I discovered that he actually loved another woman. I really couldn't stand that, and since then I have never been happy with him. I will never forget it, never. And believe me, if I hadn't had my children with him, I would rather be alone. When you live alone, you don't need to be responsible. Now, I feel I am missing a lot. I don't like him as a husband, and when he comes to me, it is as if it is out of pity or sympathy, not love. I consider him a sick person and that is not a good feeling between husband and wife. But the children love him. They play with him when they come home from kindergarten. It would be impossible for me to separate them, because I know I would not be happy if I did. I would feel that I had hurt my children and that would be my responsibility. But when they are over 18, I will ask them for permission to live alone, and if they say it is all right and that it won't hurt them psychologically, I will do it.

I am fond of my husband as a friend, nothing more. I lost my love for him forever. He can never make me feel it again. Once it is destroyed, it is destroyed. Maybe there is something wrong with me, but in my family we cannot accept sharing a man with another woman. I can't accept that a man lives with me with his body, while he lives with another woman with his feelings. I feel he likes to live with me because I am a good person, not because I am a good wife. He can go to bed with me, for example, and have an orgasm with me as a body, but not as a special woman, which I am. He also suffers a lot. When he asks me: "Did I make you happy?" I answer: "No." Then he becomes angry and says: "Why did you do it then?" I think of it in a very logical way. If I refuse to do it with him – now we do it once every one or two months – if I say: "I will never do it with you again," then it will be very bad for our family. It will affect the children.

I discuss it with myself. I say: "On the one hand, it is impossible to be divorced from this man because of the children. On the other hand, you must also think of yourself." Only little things make me happy now, nothing else. But then again, I think: "The children did not choose to come into the world. I brought them here. I am responsible for my mistakes. I chose their father, and I must pay for my guilt." My sister chose to be divorced, and I can see how it affected her daughter. I can also see it in the Danish families around me. (Middle East)

The insoluble conflicts between the sexes also exist in the West. 'In our society, women are oppressed, exploited and underprivileged', writes the

German sexologist Gunter Schmidt (1989). He emphasizes that we all, both women and men, associate sex with danger, a danger that contains:

> fear of involving oneself and thereby becoming dependent. Fear of giving of oneself and thereby losing oneself. Fear of losing control and thus becoming vulnerable. Fear of committing oneself and thereby risking being deserted. Fear of the wishes, also the burning wishes – and also fear of being left alone with them. All these expressions of fear create anger and aggression (Ibid. p. 191).

For Western women, too, the body's orifices represent threatened or vulnerable boundaries. We have no solid social structure in the form of a binding institution of marriage to dull the fear of desertion or to give protection from too great an intimacy. Couples in the West (including those in exile) are left alone with each other and their emotions; they must try to create a compromise between the fear of losing their identity in intimacy and of being left alone in estrangement. Western women also have to deal with the conflict between the freedom to define oneself and the need for security in marriage – an institution that is in the process of disintegrating. In Sweden, too, we find the polarization of the pure and elevated mother figure and the unclean and despised hetaera figure. In the Western Daughter's Room, the first and second bleeding symbolize a psychological rather than a social process, and also give a warning: now you must 'be careful' about sexuality. Perhaps women must be more careful about the psychological dangers inherent in committing their identity and self-respect to one man – now that men no longer are duty-bound to support their wives economically. On the other hand, to be too careful can militate against the development of an intimate and committed relationship. As the Swedish author Kerstin Ekman comments in her book, *The Knife Thrower's Woman*, a woman must have self-esteem: 'She must be so sure of herself that she does not duck. Therefore, she must, at one and the same time, be careful, watch out for herself and respect herself. That is the female dilemma.'

These women in The Daughter's Room have reacted differently to the meanings attached to blood. Some have accepted them, but the majority have attempted to rebel, either then or now. But it is difficult not to be involved in blood's bonds and in its ambiguities. Anything that endangers the accepted order is labelled unclean and shameful. Impurity seeps unnoticed into body and soul. That is the *power of shame*.

3. The Father's Room

We have come from a space defined by the girl's bodily changes and their
psychological and social significance. Our aim was to understand how these
changes and their symbolism contribute to forming her experience of
womanhood and sexuality. We heard about various forms of control over
women's sexuality – power strategies to ensure that the girl accepts and
fulfils her function in the private sphere of the woman's house. We saw these
power strategies as elements in an almost unconscious *structural violence*
embedded in the cultural and social structure itself, which simultaneously
contributes to maintaining this structure and the existing distribution of
power.

In The Father's Room, we turn the prism and look into another space
that defines a girl's life in a male-centred universe. We continue the theme
of structural violence, but now turn to an 'illegitimate' and shadowy side of
this violence – the narrative of male transgressions. This is a narrative about
sexual abuse of girls. It is a narrative about the 'patriarchy' which has
crossed the line and drawn its own marginal area too far out: on the one
hand, these sexual transgressions express some inherent contradictions in
the social control of women's sexuality; on the other, they can be seen as a
sign that this control has run wild and begun to undermine its own
foundation. These stories illustrate one more expression of the ambiguities
assigned to the category of 'woman': the pure and the impure; madonna and
whore; human being and symbol of exchange; value and sign (Douglas 1966;
Lévi-Strauss 1968).

The narrative of The Father's Room is about sexual aggression in the
public and *private* spaces, about experiences on the street, traditionally a
male domain, and within the home, traditionally a female domain. Some of
these stories are episodes which any girl may experience in Western society
too.

In the public space

> In my country, it is very common to be subject to assault as a child, without actually being raped. You have to be alert all the time. Even if you just get on the bus, you have to defend yourself so nobody touches your ass. All women in my country have experienced that kind of assault, because it is part of the stupid man's culture we all belong to. Men have full right to touch your ass or breasts or whatever. I remember once as a little girl a man did that. I was so angry. I shouted at him, but he just smirked. And the little boys learn it quickly. (Latin America)

Growing up in 'the stupid man's culture' puts girls on constant alert. They also learn here, in the public space, about their ambiguous status and their responsibility for watching out that others do not transgress their sexual boundaries.

> From the age of twelve, you experience many embarrassments – somebody touching you in the bus or on the street, or saying things to you. I got very angry sometimes and I cried. I think it makes you reject sexuality. You don't like it so much. You set a definite limit for how close your sweetheart can come. So there is a big distance between you. When your breasts begin to develop, boys say many things, and you feel so ashamed. My parents always said: "You be careful; you be careful. Be careful of the boys. They must not come too close or dance too close." (Latin America)

If the boundaries around you have been too well-protected, it becomes difficult to be sexually close, because that demands a temporary loss of boundaries, a letting go that can feel life-threatening for one who has learned to be constantly on the alert. And the girl is confronted with a contradiction that is difficult to solve: on the one hand, she must accept that man's closest proximity; on the other, she must not accept it.

> Once a man had to deliver a letter and wanted me to follow him. It was on a stairway. He tried, and then it seemed he changed his mind. I felt so dirty and sick. I was about nine years old. It was a man I had seen often, because he passed through our street on his way to work. I realized after a while that he knew who lived in the house, because he was well acquainted with the whole neighbourhood. I grew up there and still saw him, but I told no one. After maybe two years, I told my aunt one day when she told me that we had to be careful when we went out. I felt a need to talk about it, but felt sick when I thought about it. He had only tried to touch me. I had on a certain dress, and I wouldn't wear it after that. I

didn't like it any more. I can still remember that dress. Nothing happened, but it was dark, he closed the door and tried to lift my dress, and then as if he changed his mind he went out again. I felt it was my fault, because we were often told that we shouldn't go with anyone. I don't know whether it was because of that experience or my upbringing, but later, when I tried to relate to my husband, it was very difficult in the beginning for me to give myself to him sexually. (Latin America)

This kind of experience is so common, in the West too, that it can hardly be called sexual violation. It is something a girl must learn if she is to move about in the public space. You must be careful when you go out of the house; and if something happens to you, it is your own fault – you are an accomplice.

In a study made in Tanzania about the extent of sexual violation, many schoolgirls said they were not even conscious of the concept of 'sexual violation'. This was defined in the study as 'unwanted sexual attention' in the form of direct or indirect verbal or physical contact. These girls did not consider unwanted sexual attention to be abnormal, on the contrary, they saw it as normal, and believed that women should accept it. This study showed that 265 girls and women out of a group of 300 had experienced sexual violation on the street, at work or at home (Hashim 1990).

Once, something happened that very much affected me, when I was six or seven years old. I was out playing with some children and a boy pulled his pants down and began to act like he wanted to go to bed with me. I was very much afraid of him. When I came home, I told no one, because I knew it was bad. I am still ashamed of what happened. While I was growing up, I was always afraid of him. (Middle East)

The feeling of being an accomplice creates shame. This woman feels contaminated by that experience, even as an adult. This shame must therefore be kept secret, but fear that the boy will speak about her disgrace pursues her. In the child's world, such anxiety can dominate existence and be felt as a constant threat.

There was a fellow who lived nearby. I must have been about eight or nine years old, he gave me candy and invited me to his house. He put me in bed and touched my vagina with his fingers; he must have masturbated but I didn't know anything about that then. I didn't know what it was. But once he did it at our house, one day when my father and mother were out. They came home unexpectedly, and he rushed out of the door. They asked what he had been doing. I told them and there was a terrible fuss. They called the police and he was taken away. I knew something was wrong, but I didn't know what. Nobody explained anything to me. I was only told that I should never do it again. What was it I must not do? (Latin America)

Because of other people's reactions of anxiety and anger to sexual transgression, the girl is left with a vague sense of having done something wrong. To be with a strange man bears with it a secret danger she does not yet understand.

These quite commonplace stories from the public space of The Father's Room can, however, also be played out in another version within the private space. Such stories move us into the borderland of incest.

In the private space

Violations in the public space almost have the character of being normal and unconscious; they are simply among the conditions for moving around in this space. But in the private space, it is different. It is assumed that the girl will be safe; it is widely agreed that sexual transgression is not part of the conditions of life within this space. But when violations do happen here, they are of a much more *conscious* nature: the adult knows perfectly well that it is forbidden, and usually the child does, too. In the private space, therefore, the girl's feeling of complicity increases: when something so unusual and forbidden happens to her, it must be because of something special about her; she must be either evil or worthless. This is the only way she, as a child, can make any sense out of such an unusual experience. Violation in the private space thus increases the degree of shame and secrecy, and subsequently, the degree of traumatization. Violation within the family space disturbs the child's basic trust in the world, and creates chaos in the historically transmitted meanings of the concept of 'family'.

He was a very distant relative, and he was very old. I remember clearly when he was at our house. At first, I liked him. I wasn't very old, and he always had chocolate or other things, and I liked to sit on his lap. But later, I realized that he was acting differently. He "squeezed" me, but I couldn't understand what it meant. But even since I've grown up, I still feel badly when I think about it. I don't really know why I couldn't tell my parents about it. Perhaps because I didn't know what his behaviour meant. Maybe they wouldn't have believed it. He was their friend, and they wouldn't be able to imagine that he did that kind of thing to their daughter. And maybe they would think it was my imagination. (Middle East)

Within the private space, in the woman's house, she ought to be protected, both by her mother and by the incest taboo. It could be claimed that no sexual violation occurred, and that in any case, it had nothing to do with incest. The girl had, however, felt safe with the old man, a feeling he exploited. But if she revealed this secret, she might destroy something valuable in her own relationship to her parents. Maybe they would think that it was her own fault. She could also destroy something valuable between her parents and the old man. Transgression of her sexual boundaries leaves her in a state of conflict in which she feels responsible for the adult family members' actions and feelings.

Seen through the eyes of some Western clinicians, such a complex of emotions denotes an incestuous relationship. In the West, especially the USA, attention to the sexual violation of girls in the private space has increased, and the boundaries between the definition of incest and other forms of sexual violation have become fluid. Some consider this development to be 'incest hysteria'; others claim that the problem has now been exposed for the first time, and that we are only seeing the 'tip of the iceberg'. If, as put forward by both Lévi-Strauss and Freud, we see the incest taboo as the very prerequisite for culture, then the widespread violation of this taboo must be understood as a symptom of the dissolution of our culture – 'a loss of culture that we cannot ignore' (Hastrup & Elsass 1988, p. 105).

The Latin word *incestus* brings us deep into the universe of impurity, blood and shame. *Incestus* means impure. 'To be incestus means to be impure in the moral or religious (or cult) sense. Etymologically, incest describes a relationship that contaminates those involved' (Nielsen 1991, p. 171). A sexual relationship between family members is an extreme threat to the boundaries of the system. At least, this has been the case in the West until recently. Such a relationship is therefore connected with a severe risk of pollution and contamination and thereby also with secrecy and shame.

The studies of the extent of such violations are based on different definitions of incest, resulting in widely varying evaluations of the extent of the problem (Kutchinsky 1990). Of the 40 stories told in The Blue Room, two are about sexual violation by fathers; two are about sexual violation by other (distant) family members; and three about violations by strangers. Thus, seven out of 40 women experienced sexual violation as children inside the home; three of these were from Latin America and four from the Middle East.

Western studies of sexual violation of girls, based on responses to questionnaires given to adult women, reveal a frequency of 10 per cent to 40 per cent, varying with the definition of violation used (Kutchinsky 1990). Because of the uncertainty concerning the boundaries of the 'forbidden area', more detailed discussion of some different concepts of sexual violation in the private space is necessary. According to Kutchinsky, sexual violations in most of the studies referred to above involve isolated incidents of obscenity, proposals to do some sexual act which is rejected by the child, or brief genital contact. But even such isolated incidents can be experienced by the child as forbidden and as transgressions:

> when I was 13 or 14 years old, a well-educated person and a member of our family visited us. It was my aunt's brother-in-law. All of us children loved him. I sat with him, and he played with me, with my breasts and that sort of thing. I stayed away from home. I couldn't explain it to my mother. He kept coming to our house, and it made me very angry. When he came, I went out, to a neighbour, for example. But I was afraid to tell anyone, because that could ruin my parents' friendship with him. He dreamed of marrying me, but I would have nothing to do with him. He shouldn't come to our house, and I was frightened. Finally, I managed to tell my older sister about it, and she understood. After a while, he didn't come so often. He sent presents to the children, the biggest to me. But I felt that he was dangerous, that he was after me. I never told my mother. Later, I married another man. (Middle East)

Some clinicians do not differentiate between incestuous violations and other kinds of sexual violations against children, but believe that they are equally traumatic for the child. Others believe that there is an important difference (Trepper 1989). The bounds for what is inside and outside the family are however difficult to determine. Are the lines that should be drawn biological, psychological or social?

> I was 13 years old the first time I went to bed with a boy. It was while I was on holiday at my uncle's and aunt's house, and it was with my cousin. My aunt came in and discovered us, and there was a big fuss. That was both because it was inside the family and because I was so young. I was sent home at once. I was very frightened because they took it so hard, but fortunately my aunt never told my mother. (Latin America)

Here, we approach the conflicting forces of blood relationships: the conflict between incestuous attraction and the incest taboo. Like Freud, anthropologist Pierre Bidou (1982) believes that if such attraction did not exist, no such strong taboo would be necessary. The incest taboo is thus based on two factors: 1) a social structure, the family; and 2) sexual attraction. The incest taboo is, so to speak, born together with the family. It is not engendered by the family. The taboo and the myths attached to it do not make us forget the sexual attraction; on the contrary, the taboo constantly reminds us of the attraction, at the same time that we learn that sexuality is one thing, while its social expression is something else.

> I think I was abused by my father as a child. But what was between my father and me was never a problem until some others got mixed up in it. I was never sure what it was and what it was not before others interfered. My mother didn't interfere. One of our servant girls did, and she made use of what *she* said it was, which I am still not sure it *was*, in a very mean way. I think what she did to me for many years was worse than what my father perhaps did to me.
>
> My father died much too soon. I never was able to talk to him about it. And I can't figure out what really happened, since he isn't here. But I remember that he kissed me and played with me and things like that. Once, I talked to my sister about it, and she said he also did it with her, but maybe not in the same way. I don't think it hurt me. I think it hurt me that my father disappeared the way he did. Suddenly he wasn't there any more. He divorced my mother and married a young woman. I met him a couple of times by chance as a grown woman. (Latin America)

Uncertainty about what has actually happened is mixed with ambiguous emotions. On the one hand, she is chosen by her father, who gives her a kind of affection she does not receive from others. On the other, he transgresses the generational boundaries and treats her as an adult. Typically the child experiences very complex emotions in relation to such a father: feelings of both love and loyalty and feelings of complicity and shame. The servant girl is completely unable to understand this complexity; for her, an incestuous relationship can only be connected with complicity and shame, carelessness and impurity.

Legal definitions of incest differ from country to country. In some, it is very harshly punished, while in others it is not considered to be a crime. Nevertheless, all countries have strong moral and religious laws against incest. In Denmark, there is a law against 'crimes within the family'. Its clause regarding incest states that 'the penalty for sexual intercourse with relatives within the immediate family is six years imprisonment' (Kutchinsky 1980, p. 22). But 'the truth is that incest (understood as sexual intercourse or behaviour closely resembling sexual intercourse with close relatives) is one of the crimes most seldom committed' (Ibid. p. 23). If we return to the stories told in The Blue Room, none of the women have experienced incest as defined in the Danish law, since none have had sexual intercourse or anything closely resembling it with their fathers.

Through psychotherapeutic research and clinical work, however, a modern definition of incest has emerged. Here, in addition to biological bounds, psychological and social bounds are drawn for how we should understand 'within the family'. In this context, incest is defined as: 'any form of sexual abuse of children committed by a person who, regardless of the formal family relationship, has a parent-like relationship to the child, and who abuses this dependence in a way that results in psychological, physical or sexual injury' (Kutchinsky 1985, p. 99).

What then is happening when we speak of father–daughter incest according to this modern definition? Herman (1988, p. 180) describes it thus:

> The sexual contact typically begins with fondling and gradually proceeds to masturbation and oral–genital contact. Vaginal intercourse may not be attempted, at least until the child reaches puberty. Physical violence or threats may not be employed, since the overwhelming authority of the parent is usually sufficient to gain the child's compliance.

Nawal el Saadawi has her story about The Father's Room in the Arab world. According to her, sexual violations against girls are widespread, and she is among those who do not differentiate between incest and other forms of violation:

> Most female children are exposed to incidents of this type. . . . The male in question may be the brother, the cousin, the paternal uncle, the maternal uncle, the grandfather or even the father. If not a family member, he may be the guardian or porter of the house, the teacher, the neighbour's son, or any other man. These incidents of sexual assault may take place without any force being used. . . . Most people think that such incidents are rare or unusual. The truth of the matter is that they are frequent, but remain hidden, stored up in the secret recesses of the female child's self, since she dare not tell anyone of what has happened to her. . . . Since these sexual aggressions usually happen to children or young girls, they are forgotten through the process known as "infantile amnesia". The human memory has a natural capacity to forget what it wishes to forget, especially if related to painful incidents or accompanied by a feeling of guilt or regret. This is particularly true of certain happenings that have occurred in childhood, and which have not been discovered by anyone. But this amnesia is never complete in most cases since something of it remains buried in the subconscious, and may come to the surface for one reason or other, or during a mental or moral crisis (El Saadawi 1980, pp. 14–15).

As we have heard in the stories from The Blue Room, el Saadawi plays an important role for several of the Middle Eastern women. As young girls, they had secretly read her books behind false covers. Their meeting with her contributed to moving the first inner barriers. But we have also seen that the world el Saadawi describes is not only an Arab world, foreign to us.

According to anthropologist Dorothy Willner (1983), the universal incest taboo can be seen 'in reality' as a transcultural taboo against child abuse, because the father concept in both Western and other cultures is expanded to include many other adults. She sees incest as an expression of the patriarchy 'running wild', 'going too far' (Ibid. p. 143): by not adhering to the patriarchal norm, incest tells us also something about that norm: women are sexual objects for men, and if no other objects are at hand, daughters can also be used. That is Leila's experience in the next story about a sexualized father–daughter relationship.

The meeting with Leila

Leila is a well-educated woman from the Middle East. She had only a few months left to complete her university education in mathematics, when she had to flee her country. 'Maybe I wasn't so interested in mathematics', Leila tells me, 'but I always wanted to prove that women are not just something to be cultivated as beautiful objects. And I have also always wanted to do something that was meaningful for society. I like to challenge everything I don't believe in.' That is the beginning of our journey into Leila's story. When we talk about her childhood, Leila starts by drawing an idealized picture of her father:

> Sometimes I think that I don't come from an ordinary family. In the first place, my father was a political person, and the government imprisoned him for it. I can't remember the period when he was in prison. But I felt the effects of it on my family. I greatly respect him, because he taught us to be democratic and listen to other people's ideas and not say: "I am right and everyone else is wrong." He taught us to believe in nothing that couldn't be proved. That was good for me when I tried to liberate myself from the Islamic way of thinking.

Leila spoke about her father, mother and siblings for a long time. I then asked her, as I asked all the other women in The Blue Room, whether as a child she had any sexual experiences with adults that she felt were disagreeable. Leila reacts violently to this question. 'I won't talk about it', she says, gets up and runs out of The Blue Room. She goes into the next room and cries, but shortly she returns. When she enters the room again, she looks angry and determined:

> It is our morality that makes them do it. It really isn't good. If you live under pressure, then it comes out in a very bad way, and you do things

because of this pressure inside you that has been building-up for many years. And what makes me continue my life with my husband – I can't respect him – is that it is not under his control. And even though I have spoken with him about it, I don't have a good opinion of men. I respect women much more. What makes me continue my life with my husband is the thought that it is not under his control or other men's. They can't control it. Maybe the same would happen to me if I were a man.

Leila then relates that as a young girl, she was subjected to incestuous advances by her father. Her father came to her at night and did 'sexual things' with her. I try to understand what she is saying by asking her some general questions about the extent of incest in her country. Leila formulates her interpretation of the causes of incest: 'It is caused by men's biological nature and the social bonds on their sexuality.' She also believes it is very widespread. I ask her if anyone speaks about it. 'No', she says, 'nobody speaks about it. It is not easy to speak about these things', she says hesitantly. I ask her whether she feels it is wrong that nobody speaks openly about these things.

Yes, but you cannot begin by talking about it in our society. You have to do many other things first, and then finally you will reach that point where we will talk about it. But it is impossible for you and me to begin with that, because the door is closed. But I talked about it with some women in my family. And they talked first about other things, until they trusted me. What they said was that they had suffered very much because of it, and that they wished their husbands would just be their friends and no more than that. They didn't like it.

At this point in Leila's story, it is unclear whether 'it' is incest, sexuality in general, or a mixture. So I ask her whether they also suffer because of what happened between them and their fathers. 'Yes', Leila answers, 'some of them have experienced that – with fathers, older brothers, uncles, sometimes grandfathers. Can you imagine that?' she asks, and she continues:

But when you reach adulthood and you believe that all that bad past is over and will never return, then all the bad does return: women don't like to make love with their husbands. They feel that something from the past influences the future, and want most of all to begin a new life. A clean life. That's what they say, but of course that's not right. Because what is clean and what is dirty? Another thing is that they don't want girls, because they believe the same will happen to them. In some families, they try to protect daughters against the father. That's why most of our women are nervous. We can't relax. We are afraid all the time. But I have to figure it out. What is wrong with men? Why do they do it, even in a developed country like Denmark with information about sex, and where they can have relationships outside marriage. Why do they do it with their daughters?

I try to communicate my point of view, but she does not accept it. Her explanation is biological. 'And therefore', she says, 'I don't feel that I can continue living with my husband. I don't believe that he is personally guilty. But all men are the same.' Later, Leila says: 'I believe that because of what happened to me – I don't like to talk about it – I have withdrawn from my husband.'

Leila's story is full of shadowy points. But she struggles against letting herself be 'cultivated like a beautiful object'. She will challenge everything she 'doesn't believe in'. She fights an inner struggle against letting the power of shame rule her – because as she says, 'What is clean and what is dirty?' She will be a human being and not an object of exchange. She will retain her right to her ambiguity. For her, just as for her sisters in The Blue Room, the fight against structural violence also becomes a rebellion against *organized violence*: the violence of the dictatorship.

4. The Cell

I have a debt to settle with my government. There is blood between them and me. Because they killed my brother, and they killed my nephew. And because my mother is dead, and because my little child is now gone. And also because they punished my other brother for two years. There is so much blood between them and me, and therefore I will never forget them. (Middle East)

Until now, we have heard about the blood that symbolizes the transition from one social existence to another, the blood that symbolizes the transition from girl to woman and carries with it the possibility of fertility, of new life. This blood is associated both with something beautiful, positive and pure and with something disturbing, secret and impure. These negative or dangerous qualities of blood have to do with the dangers surrounding sexuality and the man–woman relationship. The danger contains a reminder to 'be careful' not to transgress the social boundaries.

But the blood 'between them and me' which the woman speaks of when telling her story in The Blue Room has another symbolic value. It is the blood that symbolizes a transgression of the boundary between life and death. While the girl's 'first' and the man's 'second' blood bore witness to life, this blood bears witness to death. A foreign power, the power of the dictatorship, has forced a transgression of the boundary between life and death, and has done this in a way that is bloody and unnatural.

Just as there is an ambiguity in the symbolism associated with life's blood, which also contains dangerous and even deadly elements (the girl could be killed if there was no blood after the wedding night), there is also another life-giving aspect of the blood of death: 'I will never forget them', she says. This statement expresses anger, revenge, determination and rebellion against injustice.

On our journey to the past, we have now travelled from the illegitimate boundary transgressions of The Father's Room down into the space which is the decisive turning point of this narrative. It was the encounter with The Cell that turned the women in The Blue Room into refugees. This encounter changed their lives decisively. In the space of The Cell, we encounter death and sexuality in a mixture which is just as common as wars. In this space, transgressions are no longer forbidden, but are part of a more or less deliberate strategy of power which aims to maintain or reinforce a certain political system. In the space of The Cell, violence is practised in public outside of its walls, and privately within its walls. Public violence outside the walls of The Cell has – as also in the space of The Father's Room – a more 'self-evident' character than the violence within its closed privacy. Behind the secret walls of The Cell, forms of violence are practised which outrage fundamental conceptions of humanity and culture.

Outside the walls

It is a wonder that rebellion can exist at all within the power system. Evidently, it is not possible to discipline human beings completely. In his book *Discipline and Punish*, Foucault (1979) analyses a society which has a prison-like structure. With this pessimistic picture, he is thinking of his own society, but his analysis is probably more relevant for our understanding of a totalitarian state and of the power strategies of a dictatorship. Such a state attempts to create a disciplined person who is both a product and a tool of those in power. People's bodies and energies are subjected to many different kinds of prison-like methods, and even their ways of *thinking* become part of the strategy of power. But despite this, Foucault (1979, p. 308) concludes with a touch of optimism, 'We must hear the distant roar of battle' in the midst of this almost total repression.

> My father was a farmer, and I remember that even as a child I was very upset about the oppression under which farm workers lived. I had already had some conflicts with my father when I was eleven, because he owned the land the others worked and I thought he was unjust toward them. I never forgot the time the father of a sick child came to ask permission to take the child to the city. He was not allowed to, and I can remember listening to that man with the sick child, who himself was a grown person. I can also remember that when he was gone, I went out and had a big fight with my father. I thought it was terribly unjust. My mother was a teacher, and even though she belonged to a privileged class, she was very conscious that this was not right. There were some people who worked very hard, and there were others who took the rewards of their labour. (Latin America)

Evidently, the roar can come from a child who meets injustice. She has not yet learned that the words of those in power about justice and human rights are simply rhetoric – a beautiful idea that does not exist in reality. The child is brought up to share with others and not be egoistic:

> I got my political convictions because I saw injustice. Even when I was very small, I could sense the differences. I, myself, did not feel poor, but once for example, when I had a new dress, I felt so ashamed in front of

some people who lived in a very poor house in our neighbourhood, even though I was proud of having a new dress. But I remember feeling shame for having such a fine, new dress. I remember the feeling, and I thought: "Why do I have a new dress, and that other girl doesn't?" (Latin America)

But in order for the distant roar of battle to grow stronger, it is necessary to organize, to create 'dangerous mixtures'. That must be stopped, and one of the techniques used by those in power is *branding*, says Foucault. You are dangerous; you have no rights:

There is still a large part of my family living in my homeland. I have made a family tree. They have provoked us so much that we need to keep digging in our past to find our identity. Their greatest provocation is that they try to deny us our identity as a people with rights. But we know that we are fighting against an international enemy much stronger than we are. (Middle East)

But, continues Foucault (p. 30), a 'soul' inhabits a person 'and brings him to existence, which is itself a factor in the mastery that power exercises over the body. The soul is the effect and instrument of a political anatomy; the soul is the prison of the body'. The struggle to remain free of this 'political anatomy' is thus extremely demanding, and you must devote your whole life to it: 'I consider myself to be, first and foremost, a political being; everything else comes after that. The political side is my whole life.' (Latin America)

And even when united against the power of the dictatorship, there is the masculine power to fight against:

In the mountains, we learned to fight against soldiers. Sometimes we worked to get food and build a few houses, and we gathered firewood. In the summer, we lived in tents, and in the winter, we lived in the small houses we built ourselves, because in the winter it is very cold, colder than in Denmark. This was not normal for women, because this was the first time that our women bore weapons. There were of course fewer women than men, and not all the men treated us well. Some had the wrong ideas. There were many conflicts between us. (Middle East)

In The Blue Room, more than half the Middle Eastern and almost all the Latin American women said that before exile they had, to varying degrees, been politically active, but the form their struggle took was limited by the conditions existing for their sex:

I did not like the regime, but I had to be careful because I had children. It was very difficult for me to be active. I was a teacher, and when they came and said that we should do something or other, I was afraid to say what I thought. I wouldn't get directly mixed up in politics. For example, they kept saying that women should wear kerchiefs in class. In my class, there were only girls, so I didn't think it was necessary for them to sit in class with kerchiefs and everything in 100° of heat. So I gave them permission to take them off. The school inspector found out and was very angry; I was called in to the Ministry of Education to explain why I had done that. They thought I had done something very bad. I told them that I didn't think it was necessary for the girls in my class to wear kerchiefs when it was so warm, and that I, their teacher, was also a woman. If I had been a man, it would have been different. But they would not accept that. So we always had these discussions, but it was not direct political engagement. I believed that the government was unjust, but I wouldn't get mixed up in it, because I didn't feel I had any power. They wouldn't listen to me, because I was the only one who said anything. Many of the other teachers agreed with me, but they kept their mouths shut. No one stood by me because they were afraid. But if something happened to the students that I felt was not right, then I said something, and if they threw me out of school, then OK. I was prepared to stay home and do something else. Finally, they punished me by sending me to a new school an hour's drive away on the other side of the mountains. In the winter, it was very cold and icy, with deep snow, the road was very dangerous and many people died. So I had to rent a room in a house in the winter and couldn't come home every day to my children, only on the weekend. I worked there one year and then we fled. (Middle East)

As Foucault says (Ibid. p. 215), power can neither be identified with a certain institution nor with a certain apparatus; it comprises a whole set of instruments, techniques, procedures, levels of application, and targets.

I was home the day the soldiers came to our house. I was afraid and crept under the table, and I saw how my mother talked to the soldiers, and my little sister – she played and laughed. The soldiers asked my mother: "Where is your brother?" My mother became frightened and couldn't answer. "I don't know," she answered finally. "What do you mean, you don't know?" said the soldiers, and they shot my mother and my little sister. My mother lay there, and I cried and ran and told my uncle about it. He cried and tore at his hair and hit himself on the head. "Come with me," I said. And we saw that my mother was dead. That was very, very common in my country. I was 14 when it happened. (Middle East)

Those in power often use more visible and gruesome techniques than the mild forms of exercising power with which we have been familiar in the West – until the war in former Yugoslavia. All the women in The Blue Room had been exposed to the power techniques of a dictatorship and, with one exception, all had been either subjected to severe abuse themselves or been witness to the abuse of those closest to them.

Among the visible attacks of those in power is the confrontation with 'the great spectacle of physical punishment', as Foucault calls it. In this political theatre of terror, pain is exhibited to the public. The transition to a more refined era for the art of punishment has not yet occurred in this story from the Middle East:

Once, I also saw how they tied one of my uncles – he was a partisan – to a truck with ropes around his wrists, and then dragged him behind it. Afterwards he was hanged. They forced us all to watch in order to frighten us into not becoming partisans. After that, I was in hospital for a month and I was completely crazy. I shook and laughed and cried. That happened in my home town. They tell us it is not our country; they murder us; many of us have fled to Europe. Many young boys live alone without their sisters or mothers. I often wonder how they are. (Middle East)

In 1986, a World Health Organization (WHO) working group introduced the concept 'organized violence' to describe societal violence, defined as the conscious and deliberate infliction of pain and suffering by an organized group according to a declared or implied strategy and/or system of ideas and attitudes (van Geuns 1987). The WHO group emphasized that violence also can be psychological. The heartbeat can be stopped by other means than a bullet:

After I had fled to some members of my family, they came and asked for me every day. They wanted to put me in prison. Finally, they came to arrest my father and he died of a heart attack. So instead, they put my mother and aunt in prison, interrogated them for seven hours and subjected them to psychological torture. They demanded that my mother swear that she would turn me over to the police if she found out where I was; and if she didn't, she would be imprisoned instead. Finally, she signed the papers. It is very hard for my family, because the police ask about me all the time. Therefore, I can't write to them. I feel very badly because my father died because of me, and because of me my whole family has terrible problems. My mother always says it is my fault that all these problems have come – because I got involved in politics. She can't forgive me. She doesn't blame the regime. (Middle East)

The WHO group's definition of societal violence points to the *conscious and systematic* infliction of suffering – that is, clear and deliberate *evil* action.

Power can use different languages, different techniques, but all are aimed at making the body docile. According to Foucault, in modern, industrialized societies, the techniques are aimed at the soul rather than the body, but the goal both of the deliberate and conscious use of violence that occurs under some dictatorships, and the hidden and unconscious use of violence that occurs under more 'refined' dictatorships, is the same: a psychological process in which the power relationship is internalized. One weapon in the resistance to these strategies of power is to expose them. By publicly denouncing the techniques of those in power, the psychological internalization of the power relationship is counteracted. The inner psychic mechanism that allows power to function automatically, so that the oppressed 'becomes the principal of his own subjection', as Foucault expresses it, is challenged. The fugitives must begin to develop their own science of power.

The Chilean human rights group CODEPU (1989) has therefore sought to make the dictatorship's violence visible by analysing its components. Violence can be classified in two main groups: direct and indirect repression. *Direct repression* includes such phenomena as: assassination; kidnapping; disappearance; detention; torture; exile; internal exile (relegation); house searches without a warrant; intimidation (surveillance and continuous harassment).

> In the nine months I lived in the transit country, I didn't have one decent night's sleep. I was always afraid someone would come and knock on the door and take my husband and my son. It was like that in all the other transit countries we lived in. And you know how it is in my homeland. (Middle East)

This is life in the space of terror. Power can force entry any time and no boundaries are safe. Reality for some is that their husbands are taken and killed:

> I am not sure how it happened. But there must have been someone who gave my name to the police. I don't know who. I think I know, but I'm not sure. So they went after my boyfriend. He also studied at the university, but he was not politically active. He lived outside the city. The police came out to the little town where he lived and picked him up together with nine other students. They were all shot down in the street, including my boyfriend. I had to go underground after that. The police came to the university. We continued working for a while in secret, even

though the repression at that time was so harsh that we had almost no contact with each other. (Latin America)

One of direct repression's most horrible weapons is to make a person *disappear* completely:

Nine months after the coup, he went to work and was supposed to return home about two or three in the afternoon. But he didn't come. I waited a few hours, and then I began to ask around all the places where he might have been. It turned out he had never arrived at work. I don't know how it happened; I'll never find out. We said "good-bye" to each other and then he went. None of the authorities will explain what happened. Two years ago, I received a letter signed by a judge stating that he died in prison, otherwise I could not have had custody of our son. But then I didn't know that so many people had disappeared. You are in the middle of all that, and you see without seeing and hear without hearing. (Latin America)

In Latin America, 'disappearance' was a widely used power technique, either through kidnapping people who were never found or by murdering them and refusing to acknowledge their deaths. The media never gave information about the disappeared. 'There was absolute silence. Silence was imposed as an official, repressive rule' (Kordon & Edelman 1988, pp. 27–28). In Argentina, the impact of this silence order even affected groups that were politically active. It was either implicitly or explicitly forbidden to refer to anything about those who were missing, and the social pressure was so strong that anyone who broke the silence order was considered a disrupting element and immediately felt excluded from the group. In the following story about a man who simply disappears out of the system, we hear how this silence and denial can happen. The murdered man is isolated in the hospital. The waiting room is emptied. No one must see, no one must hear – and no one will see or hear:

I received a telephone call from my former work place; they said the police had been there, three men. They had asked what I was doing, my political ideas, who were my friends, and if I was politically active. They had also looked for me at my former apartment. So I thought: "Now, it is serious!" I hadn't thought that before. My boyfriend had said we had better leave home, because they would probably come sooner or later. I was just packing our things when I heard the police come. We lived in a long room with some partitions across it. I was in the furthest part, which was very narrow, a large closet with a small entrance. I think that was why they didn't find me. That is the only explanation. I was in there, on the other side of the partition getting some clothes. What happened was my fault. My boyfriend had said we should leave at once, but I insisted we should take some clothes. We couldn't just leave without anything. But then I heard a voice say: "The man is from the police." It was my uncle's voice. "The man is from the police." I thought he was just saying that so I would hurry, but a second later I heard a stranger's voice asking: "Are there other rooms in the house?" "Yes," my uncle answered. "We have an apartment upstairs." "Oh," said the policeman, "then we'll go up there." Then I heard many steps. I think that is why they didn't find me. Just before the police came, my boyfriend had said that if they did come, I should run and he would stay. But I said, "no", and he repeated that I should run. "The police might beat me," he said, "but you are a woman and everyone knows that the police rape and torture women." That was something we all knew. While the police were upstairs, I managed to get out of the apartment. In the street, I saw a blue-grey car – the kind we knew belonged to the police. I was sure that the driver would shoot me, but they were all upstairs. But I kept expecting to get a shot in the back. When I reached my girlfriend's, I began to call home. I called and called. No one answered for an hour except once when it was them that picked up the phone and I put down the receiver. But finally my uncle answered. He said: "I think they have killed him." I went home immediately, completely oblivious of the risk I was taking. He wasn't dead, so I took him to the hospital. He was unconscious. We had big windows and my uncle could see how inhumanly they beat him. When he fell, one of them jumped up and down on his chest. He had been tortured, that was the cause of his death. It was very hard to find anyone who would drive us to the hospital. I asked three of our neighbours who had cars but none of them dared. Finally, I saw a stranger on the street and told him what happened, that we had to get to a hospital – and he said: "I'll help you." At the hospital, they put him in a room alone, because I told them what had happened. A doctor came in to see him and determined that there was internal bleeding. "We can't do anything for him," he said. Suddenly, I had to go to the toilet and while I was there – until then I hadn't been able to think normally, I was in total shock. I had in fact asked the doctor what would happen now, and he had said: "We will call the police and tell them what has happened." I had been so shocked that I hadn't thought about it. When I came out of the toilet, it suddenly hit me that the police were actually looking for me, not him. So what was I doing here? That was the first time I saw my situation from the point of view of survival, and so it was clear that I had to get out of there. I was at the hospital and the police would come. I went out through the emergency waiting room which was usually full of people, and now suddenly no one was there. I simply walked out onto the street and disappeared. So his body remained there. I read and read the newspapers but I never found a word about his death. (Latin America)

The silence order is an essential ingredient of *indirect repression*. The silence order is part of the censorship and the systematic manipulation of information that belong to the indirect techniques. Others are (CODEPU 1989): dismissal from work; deprivation of housing, health services, food; severance from social, political and labour associations; total or partial loss of individual and collective freedom of expression, sometimes imposed under the pretence of legal principles, sometimes through self-censorship provoked by fear.

All these strategies were included in the above story. And people continue to flee:

We revolutionary students were no longer allowed to participate in classes. My husband was imprisoned, but released under the amnesty. We were forced to live illegally anyway, because of the situation. We fled from place to place every week, and many times it was evening and we didn't know where we should go. We lived this way for a year, but gradually the situation got worse because the police were on our trail and we could no longer be politically active. Finally, we fled the country with false passports. First, we went to Sweden where we were in custody for 24 hours before they put us on a plane back to our country. But when we landed in Copenhagen, we ran to the police to seek asylum. Here, we were also immediately imprisoned because we had false passports. We were in prison for 24 days. (Middle East)

Those in power create 'institutions of repression, rejection, exclusion, *marginalization*' (Foucault 1979, p. 308, my emphasis). CODEPU (1989) describes this process as two-phased: *social marginalization* in which the one persecuted loses his or her social and political power, and *individual marginalization* accompanying the social marginalization as a consequent psychological state. This state is characterized by an increasing breakdown of self-esteem because of forced passivity and isolation. The illegal existence experienced by most of the women in The Blue Room illustrates both forms of marginalization:

I was wanted by the police, and my parents received a letter from the Islamic Court that I had been expelled from the university because I had been politically active there. The letter also said that I should report to the prison for questioning. They wrote: "If you are innocent, we will help you and you will be released. But if you are guilty, then you must serve our God by going to prison." I knew that I would never return if I reported to the prison because that had happened to others. So my comrades and I decided that none of us would report. We didn't care about our education or anything else. In any case, we weren't going to prison, so we all went underground. Those who could, moved to another part of the country – for example, those whose parents knew someone or had a large family living elsewhere who could hide them. My parents rented an apartment for me and my sisters and we lived there for a year without anyone knowing who we were. Every weekend my parents came with food. It wasn't so easy to live like that. The neighbours must not know who we were, and we could not speak to anyone. (Middle East)

It is difficult not to privatize, to internalize such a political assault. The persecuted person seeks an explanation of the painful experience, and in the same way as in the private space of The Father's Room, easily finds an explanation in some weakness or indignity in oneself. The feeling of complicity starts to grow: 'It was almost like a circle that closed around you. Finally, you didn't have any place to stay, to sleep. I ran from place to place. And I felt guilty about having left everything.' (Latin America)

The direct and indirect power techniques include, to a certain degree, an attempt to camouflage violence. Surveillance is, in the words of Foucault, 'like a faceless gaze that transformed the whole social body into a field of perception: thousands of eyes posted everywhere' (Ibid. p. 214), but in open war there is no longer any attempt to hide the face of power, and life becomes a constant flight from death:

In the ten years I was married, I only lived in my own house, if you add up all the days, for two years. Every day we had to escape to other places to protect ourselves from bombs and attacks. This affected my son especially and every night he awoke with a kind of hysterical fit and ran outside and shouted and cried. Finally, I realized that if I didn't leave the country, I would lose my son. I clearly remember the winters – the weather was so terrible, but we had to leave the house and find shelter for ourselves and the children. When they bombed us, we left the camp and went into the city, because they only bombed the camp, never the city. And when they were fighting in the city, we fled back to the camp. That was our life. It started in 1982 and it never stopped. (Middle East)

A paradoxical feeling of guilt develops about surviving while others die. This 'survivor guilt' (Ochberg 1988) makes existence in relatively secure exile an experience full of conflict. Anxiety about the family remaining in the homeland goes hand-in-hand with these guilt feelings:

I don't remember much from that time. It really took a long time for my memory to come back, and I first began to be conscious of my anxiety when I came to Denmark. It was an anxiety that suffocated me, and it could come anytime. I felt as if I had to be in bed all the time. I was ill. It was probably because I couldn't stand the thought that now I was a refugee living in exile. Maybe it would have been better if I had been in prison all those years. I felt defeated. I didn't feel I had any reason to be a real refugee. I felt that others needed that safety much more than I did. I felt guilty. Guilt has been a characteristic all the way through. I felt insufficient. I felt: "why do I live? Why me, when many of the others I was close to died?" It's hard for me to say this. It's difficult to find words – both in Danish and Spanish. I felt as if it were too much to be given asylum in Denmark and live so well, knowing that others were in such bad circumstances. (Latin America)

The Middle Eastern women tell about the wounds of war. The face of power is crippling, and even the future is taken from the people:

The war started when I was eleven. I remember we ran out into the woods when they began to bomb our town. We sat under the trees and saw their tanks drive right by us. Of course, we were very frightened because we had heard all kinds of stories about the last time they attacked our country. They had killed whole villages and raped the women. So we were very frightened that the same would happen to us. I had no desire to think about the future then. It was war all the time, and you never knew when you also would be killed. The future was dark. (Middle East)

Inside the walls

For some people, the persecution in public space also leads to detention in the closed 'privacy' of the prison. The prison can be seen as an image of the outer world. Some of the power techniques we have already met in The Daughter's Room and The Father's Room are recreated in the prison in concentrated form. The prison is, as Foucault (1979 p. 231) expresses it, 'the penalty *par excellence*'. In prison, a person can be both marginalized and branded. In his analysis of power, Foucault finds that marginalization and branding are the two basic forms of exercising power. These two forms of exercising mastery over people can be exemplified historically by examining how those in power in various societies dealt with leprosy and plague. Lepers were isolated from society, whereas those infected by the plague were classified and branded:

The exile of the leper and the arrest of the plagued do not bring with them the same political dream. The first is that of a pure community, the second that of a disciplined society. Two ways of exercising power over men, of controlling their relations, of separating out their dangerous mixtures. (Ibid. p. 198)

In this narrative, we meet both 'the exile of the leper and the arrest of the plagued'. The plagued or the *impure* are confronted, inside the walls of The Cell, with their private and political contamination. Three-quarters of the women in The Blue Room have experienced imprisonment – either their own or that of those closest to them. And in prison, the power of the dictatorship penalizes with both physical and psychic death:

My aunt's children all belonged to the same political group and they were all arrested. They executed my 24-year-old girl cousin and another has been in prison for seven years. My youngest cousin – she was 14 then – was also arrested and severely tortured. Afterwards, they sentenced her to life imprisonment – a 14-year-old girl! But my aunt and her husband were able to buy her freedom. They paid a very large sum to the prison. They succeeded in freeing her because she was so young. She hadn't done anything. She had only been to a demonstration; that was all. So she is free now, if you can call it that. . . . (Middle East)

In the prison of the dictatorship, torture is executed. It is systematic and deliberate. It is, in Foucault's (1979, p. 198) words, 'a technique; it is not an extreme expression of lawless rage'. Torture is a widely used power technique, one form of power among others.

There is a tendency to see torture as something inhuman, perverse and rare. The truth is that torture is one of the most 'human' things we know of, since this form of exercising power has been part of human relations at least since the ancient Egyptians (Suedfeld 1990). But besides being a power technique, torture is also an art form: 'Torture rests on a whole quantitative art of pain. But there is more to it: this production of pain is regulated' (Ibid. p. 34):

The worst was that while we felt so awful, doctors and nurses would come and examine us and take our blood pressure and pulse. And they said to the soldiers: "you better be careful of that one." We could peek out under our blindfolds so we could recognize their shoes, and there was one nurse who had some really fine sandals – I will always remember her. She came over to me after I had signed a confession. I had to write it myself, and if they thought it was good enough, I could sign it and be released. Otherwise, they would make one themselves and I should just sign it. But then that nurse came and said: "You are so dumb. Why don't you tell everything you know? That is much better." I hated her and her sandals. (Latin America)

Torture is an extreme expression of the coupling of the two basic forms of power: leprosy's marginalization and the plague's branding. Those in power seek through their agents (the torturers) to turn their victims (their opponents) into lepers or carriers of the plague. The fact that victims are viewed in this way is a psychological explanation of how torturers are able to perform their handiwork. The victims (those in opposition) are not human; they are monsters, scum (Staub 1990).

I was completely unprepared for what would happen in prison. We had too little information about how it was. They talked a lot about the torture, but it is not only the torture. It is also the blindfold, not having any sense of time or place. You didn't know how large or small was the room you were in, and they did little evil things to you. For example, when you were supposed to walk, they would say: "be careful of the step." And there was no step. You not only felt powerless, you felt like a little child, without your senses. And like a little child, you began to develop your senses bit by bit. Your sense of hearing was gradually sharpened. But you never knew what was going to happen to you – when they would let you sleep, when you could get something to eat. So it wasn't only the electrical torture. It was everything. We had only heard about what they did to you, that they could stub a cigarette out on your arm. But all the other things were even worse. Not knowing what could happen to you – the psychological things. It is much more important to know how to survive that. I remember there were some who began to scream because they felt so desperate and helpless in that situation. (Latin America)

In a disturbing way, some psychological and medical research about torture can come to support the power's marginalization and branding of its victims. It is actually common to describe torture as a sickness in the society. The introduction to one of the newest theoretical works on psychology and torture starts with the sentence: 'There is growing evidence that torture is *epidemic* throughout major parts of the world (and *endemic* in some countries)' (Suedfeld 1990, p. xv – my emphasis). And doctors investigate 'the medical aspects of torture'. An attempt is made to 'prevent' torture by classifying and listing its various medical and psychological *symptoms* – just as the powers once did in relation to the plague. 'Torture victims' are isolated and marginalized by being 'treated' at special centres. All these methods can help to increase humiliation and political passivity.

But torture is not a monstrous illness. It is common and widely used in the exercise of power practised in one-third of the countries of the world (Stover & Nightingale 1985), and its use is constantly increasing (Engdahl & Eberly 1990). Torture is, paradoxically enough, both interrogation and penalty, and it must be understood as a political ritual: 'It is an element in the liturgy of punishment and meets two demands': It must mark and brand the victim, and it must have a terrorizing effect (Foucault 1979, p. 34).

Let us now hear Ana's story about this political ritual, a story that is not at all unusual. In common with all survivors of human rights violations, she expresses the conflict between denying the traumatic experience and telling the truth about it to the world.

The meeting with Ana

'My children and I were fugitives the whole time,' Ana begins. 'I was also arrested. I can't really remember it. It was so long ago, and I never think about those things. When my daughter was two years old, I was arrested. It was not only because of my husband. I had my own political work. At that time, together with my sister, we hid fugitives. Both my sister and I had been active as students and at work, so we knew many people in the opposition. All the organizations and infrastructures had been destroyed, so we had to rely on the work of individuals. All the organizations' contact people had either been arrested or murdered or kidnapped, so the people who knew each other, and who had work, helped others who were on the street and had no place to live. So I was arrested. And when I was released, I never thought it would happen. Suddenly, I was released.'

'But you were arrested?' I ask.

'Yes,' Ana says.

'When did that happen?'

'Lisa was 11 months old. It was in October – the beginning of October. The third or fourth of October, 1974. I remember that. That day.'

'How did it happen?'

'What?' Ana asks.

'How did the arrest happen?'

'In the middle of the night. It was three or four in the morning. It was very cold, they knocked and knocked and knocked. And when I opened the door, I thought I saw a man with a beard. I thought it was my husband, and I held the door wide open. I was . . . I knew they would come. I always knew it, because it was much too lucky that I had worked so long without anything happening. So I opened the door and thought it was my husband. Yes, I knew perfectly well it wasn't him, but when you feel alone with your fate you can believe anything at all. The procedure was the usual. There wasn't room for so many soldiers in that little house.'

'And they destroyed everything?'

'I didn't have very much to destroy. I had always been very poor. I had only my parents' old furniture, nothing else. I had only one lamp, and I had taken that into the bathroom after bathing the children. I sat in there and wrote a letter until late at night, before they came. They thought that because the house was so poor and there was nothing much at all, it could be a hiding place for the guerrillas. Everything, my children's clothes, were torn out of the closets. Even Lisa's cradle was overturned.'

'What happened to the children?'

'Lisa didn't understand what was happening, and the only thing I can remember about Miguel was . . . I don't feel like talking about it . . . I have separated my feelings from the things that happened then. Sometimes, I can do that; other times I can't.

'They were not human. They were beasts. I don't remember very much. They held a bayonet, I think, here against my stomach, and I had a pistol pressed against my head. I can't remember how many there were. And I saw Miguel walking around with bare feet wearing only a diaper. He was no taller than their boots. And he was tramped on.' Ana cries. 'And Miguel only tried to gather some of his things. They were idiots; I'm sure they did it on purpose. I had a pile of writing paper with Miguel's drawings – at that time – I think he had started drawing circles. One of the soldiers took one of the drawings and asked: "What is this?" He was an idiot. And Miguel said: "It's mine, it's mine." I didn't really understand anything that was happening. It wasn't anything that had any . . . I didn't have anything, anything that could incriminate me there. I had only the most necessary things, and I lived alone with my two children, who were very small. Fear, anxiety . . . how should I answer all their questions. I was kicked . . . Luckily, my parents were able to come and save the children. Maybe a neighbour had called them. Otherwise, they would have arrested them with me. And that was my only support, that the children were living with my parents . . . In the car, they put a hood over my head and drove a long time, just to confuse me so I didn't know where I was. I knew anyway. I knew everything. It was as if I had eyes – a sixth sense – which told me where I was. Later, when I talked with others who had been to the same place, I confirmed that it was precisely the place I thought it was. It was an army base, and it was the army that arrested me.'

'And you went there?'

'Yes,' Ana answers. 'I was released almost immediately. I was only there 24 hours. But apparently it was enough to wound me psychologically. I was treated later by a psychologist. I went to her for a year. And sometimes, when I didn't feel so good, I called her for a consultation . . . But it was not only those 24 hours, because they were after me for a long time after that, and I was always afraid. But it was also because – and I learned that in therapy – I experienced psychological violence – all that happened while I was under arrest and later.

'I didn't know anything about that then. But that was also because I was very lucky with all the blows they gave me. I don't know how I survived without any broken bones. I knew all about what would happen.'

'You were prepared, then?'

'Yes, I was prepared. But when things happened, then it was as if you weren't prepared for anything. I knew everything, and I was given the usual welcome with kicks and blows and trips up and down stairs. It was thus I could confirm where I was. I knew that stairway from descriptions of others. It was a very famous stairway, and I had a couple of trips. And I. . . .

'After the long ride in the car, we arrived there, at the army post, and they took everything I had in my pockets, and then I had to go up the stairs, in the usual way. They beat me with their rifles, and then I sat there a long time, to soften me up. Meanwhile, I had to listen to a tape of an interrogation of a woman who was being tortured. I sat and listened to it for a long time. And then suddenly someone came and took my hood off and put a blindfold on me instead. I had to urinate but I wouldn't because there was a whole lot of soldiers around me and I was supposed to urinate in a hole there. I wouldn't, but they almost forced me. And I tried to see it. It was just a hole in the ground with nothing to sit on. I had my hands tied behind my back, so I couldn't do anything; they had to help me.'

'That was a humiliation – also a sexual humiliation?'

'I thought they would also do that – rape me, but they didn't,' Ana answers. 'Well, nothing happened; I couldn't urinate. And then I had to listen to the tape again. Then, other prisoners came. I wasn't in a cell. It was like a corridor, and there were cells. And the prisoners couldn't walk. I don't know why, but they simply couldn't walk. I couldn't see them, but I sensed it. I don't know how it happened, but at one point I saw a man – one of my fellow prisoners – a man I thought I knew. And then he asked me how I was, if my family knew where I was, and I thought I recognized him. It was a fellow I met at the university. I never was able to confirm it because I didn't know his name. But there were also other shouts; there were other prisoners. I sat sort of alone. Then suddenly, I recognized the voice of a girl whom I knew had disappeared and whom I knew well. She was a schoolteacher. Well, then I was taken to interrogation and the trip up the stairs again; I was pushed and I rolled down and was kicked and beaten. And then to the interrogation room. It was painted in a fine way. I know that because when I sat down they took the blindfold off, and there were lights everywhere, and I couldn't see because of all the strong lights. In that room, a woman was being tortured. They said that they would torture her as long as I wouldn't co-operate with them. They also said that she was my friend. I didn't know what to believe. They asked me about my husband's cover name and I said I didn't know. When I couldn't say no to a question, I said yes. When it was obvious that I must have met people sometime in my life, I said yes to knowing them, and others I denied knowing. In fact, I told them nothing. I didn't name any names or places. But something happened during that interrogation. I don't know when, but at some point, I wanted to remember certain things and I couldn't. It was as if I had lost my memory. Names and how people looked – I couldn't remember. I became confused. It's lucky, I thought: "now, I can't remember. I'm saved. They can't get anything out of me in any case." I don't know how long it lasted. I was struck on the way out of the interrogation room, and again on the way up the stairs – it was the same. Then I sat up there again and heard the tape recorder. Then, on the way down the stairs they said that now we were going for a little ride, and I thought: "that's it." I thought they were moving me to a better place to really interrogate me, or maybe make me disappear or kill me, or I don't know what. I didn't think I would see the light of day ever again. I only hoped they would kill me quickly. That was my only wish. Then, there was another long ride with a hood and handcuffs on. I was given all the things I had with me, except for the money. I didn't have very much money, but what I had was gone.

'At one point, they put me at the back of the car, and then I – yes, I must have been struck with a rifle and I was out of the car.'

'But the car drove on?'

'Yes, and I rolled over and over. And I thought, now they'll run over me, and I thought, I hope so because then I'll die quickly. But the car didn't come. Well, I thought, then they'll shoot me in the back, but they won't get that chance. I couldn't get up right away. I remember that. But when I finally did stand up, I thought that they shouldn't get the chance to shoot me in the back. So I stood up with my back against a tree and waited and waited and waited to be shot. But I wasn't. Then I put my glasses on. They weren't even broken. It was unbelievable. And I walked away. It was less than half an hour by bus from that place to where I lived. I knew the neighbourhood well. And I thought, I must find a place to call home and say that I was all right and had been released. I went into a café. I was afraid to go in. There were only men in there, lots of men. And when I came in, I looked around me, and it was as if there was complete silence. Everyone looked at me, and then I was afraid again. I went to the bar and asked the waiter if I could use the telephone, and he just stared at me. So I asked again if I could borrow the telephone, and then he said: "But what happened to you? Tell me!" I wouldn't tell him, but just repeated that I would like to use the telephone. "You can use the telephone, but what happened to you?" Then he asked me whether I wanted a cognac – something strong to drink, but I wasn't used to drinking so I said no, I only wanted a telephone. He gave me the telephone, and then he could hear that I said that I had just been released. He called another waiter who would help me get a taxi, and he asked me whether I wouldn't rest a bit and he said they would help me. That's not what I wanted to do. They asked me a whole lot of questions that I wouldn't answer. I was terrified. The only feeling I had the whole time was fear. I was afraid. I am no heroine. I am completely ordinary. I am most like – how shall I say – well, I'm afraid, and I can't hide my fear. I kept trying to hide it the whole time I was at the army post. It was as if it oozed out of me. As I say, I am no heroine, and I am not good at hiding such feelings, but there were two things I remember the soldiers saying about me. Do you know what *hija de puta* means? It can mean so many things – it depends on how you say it. Actually, it means, "daughter of a whore". And that is a humiliating name to call a woman. And the other thing they said was: "she doesn't cry." Well, I didn't cry or scream or anything. It was as if that upset them. But I was so terrified that I simply could not make a sound, and they noticed that. It was as if that was an unexpected reaction. But I was terrified, and I took them seriously. I took them really seriously. I knew this was no game. I knew that the whole time; since I started working politically I knew this was no game, that it could have serious consequences. And the worst would be just this situation in which I should stand and be interrogated without wanting to say anything, and at the same time without being able to hide my terror. I don't know what the men at the café thought. I only know that I was still terrified, and that I remained that way a long, long time afterwards.

'I couldn't fall asleep, for example, even though I was very tired. And I couldn't open my mouth. It was as if I had cramps that made me unable to open it. Many times it was hard to breathe because it was as if my jaws were locked, and that happened while I slept. Another consequence was that Miguel would have an hysterical fit every time he saw an army or police car or anyone in uniform. He screamed and shouted and cried and clung to me and shouted: "you must not go. Don't leave me alone." And that happened anywhere – in the bus, on the street, anywhere.

'But I wasn't tortured. I have pointed out that I wasn't anything special. You can't convince me of anything else, for I have close friends who were victims of real torture and therefore I don't think. . . . One of the reasons that I don't like to talk about it is that I know what torture is, and what it means to be a torture victim, and I am ashamed that I was so weak that I only had to be in there for 24 hours and that was enough to make me suffer bad nights for a long time. I am no heroine. What I feel most when I talk about it is shame.'

'What is your shame?'

'That I wasn't really tortured and that I feel like I do anyway. I think the worst was the period just afterward when I thought I was being pursued all the time.

'Some time afterwards, I was out with my children close to where we lived, in a big park. It was the middle of the day, sunshine, warm. And I took toys and books along – I liked to read – I always have. So I took the children along and there were other children there playing. I sat and read while the children played. But then suddenly, while I sat and read, I had the experience that I no longer heard the sound of the children playing. Everything seemed silent suddenly, so I looked around me. Not a child, not a soul. And by chance a strange car drove by, and I thought: "now, they are going to kidnap the children and me." Then I thought of the children, and I took them and ran home as fast as I could, and I forgot all my things in the park. I couldn't be any place where there weren't many people. I didn't dare go any place where I knew there would only be me and the children. When I was all alone, it wasn't so bad. But the problem was that I was always with my children. I was most afraid that they would disappear. It was that terror, that fear, that anxiety – that I also later experienced when I lived alone with the children after we fled. I was alone with the children. I had to protect them all the time.'

The political technology of the female body

Inside the walls of The Cell, Ana met a form of boundary-transgressing violence which we already know about from the private space of The Father's Room. But now she is in The Cell of the dictatorship. This situation is charged with confusing ambiguity. And in this space she meets torture. Just as prison can be seen as an image of the power system of society, torture also reflects common power techniques. 'The political technology of the body' reflects the body's position in the political economy. The body must be obedient, but at the same time productive. In a society with a weakly developed system of finance and production, for example, the use of physical punishment is more widespread, because the body is most often the only resource which is available to penalize. But with industrialization, the prison gradually takes over the penalizing function, and methods are developed which no longer strike at the body but at the soul (Foucault 1979).

In the prisons of the dictatorship, torture strikes at both the body and the soul. It punishes through physical suffering, and must be, in Foucault's words, 'a punishment that acts in depth on the heart, the thoughts, the will, the inclinations' (Ibid. p. 16). It must disgrace its victim by disgracing her body. But in this context, the purpose of the political technology of the body is no different. Here also, what is essential for those in power is to make human bodies both productive and submissive.

But these bodies have a gender, and in the political technology of torture gender differences are exploited. *The political technology of the female body is different.*

> I remember as a child that we sewed clothes for the partisans, and trucks came and fetched our handiwork, and brought it up to the mountains. My father had many daughters, and he was afraid that we would be politically active, for our underdeveloped society really creates many problems for girls if they are sent to prison. They will be made pregnant, and so on, and they will have many problems. Therefore, he tried to get us to go into the political world only indirectly. (Middle East)

In the *sexualization* of the political technology of the body, power techniques are used that belong to the spaces of The Daughter's Room and The Father's Room. In prison, women are in a space which belongs to both men and soldiers.

> Sexual abuse does not only happen in prisons. It also happens on the street when the police come and you have to show your identity papers. They stop you and you have to raise your hands, and then they touch you sexually. They have to touch you to search you, but they do it with something else in mind. You are very affected by it. It feels like rape. I remember one day when we were just leaving the university, they stopped us and we had nothing on us that we shouldn't, so they didn't find anything. But they came with their rifles and said we should spread our legs, and they put their rifles between our legs. At first, you don't feel so much because you are afraid. The only thing you think about is to get away. You think, why have they stopped me and what are they after. All these thoughts whirl around inside you. But later you feel badly; you can always feel what they did to you. For a long time after that, I didn't feel like having my boyfriend touch me. But it helped to talk with other women about it. There are so many women who have experienced it, and it helps to know that I am not the only one they have touched. You feel that the others understand how it was. (Latin America)

Both without and within the walls of The Cell, the techniques applied by those in power engender humiliation. The abuse in public space outside the walls of The Cell, however, has an almost 'unconscious' quality, similar to what women commonly experience when they go into the streets – into male territory. These experiences, familiar to most women, are probably more easily de-privatized because women can talk to each other about them. But inside the walls of The Cell, the power of shame is very different. The isolation there is reinforced by the blindfold and the prohibition against speaking to each other. The quality of abuse is completely different in that its focus is specifically concentrated upon each particular individual. In common with the incestuous space of The Father's Room, this is a matter of being *chosen*.

> When we came to the police station, they started to beat and kick me. And they shouted that I was shit and used a lot of swear words. They asked about weapons and such things. I had handcuffs on, and I was suspended, without clothes, by the handcuffs on some hooks. They insulted me and said: "She is ugly," and that kind of thing. Fortunately, I didn't care about that. But it offended my sense of morality that they touched me and said: "look at those long tits." At that point, I just wanted to die. I wished they would kill me. I couldn't stand it. They asked about my husband and my friends. I had heard that if you drink after electric shock, you can risk a heart attack. So I asked for a cup of coffee. And once they gave me a cup, but I only felt a little tremor. Nothing happened. I felt so ashamed. Maybe it would be different now that I have developed a lot and feel that my body belongs to me. But my mother was very Catholic, and I had gone to a Catholic school. (Latin America)

The sense of complicity is reinforced by the intimate and deliberate focus on the body which suddenly belongs to 'them' in a sexual way. By dishonouring her body they violate her *morally*. Thus, with the sexualized torture technique directed against the woman's body, those in power aim to make her 'impure'.

> I think their major objective is to make you feel like an animal. For example, when you have your menstruation they won't let you wash yourself, and it is very rare to be allowed to take a bath. So you feel – and not only feel because you simply *are* – dirty. One month without bathing or washing your hair when you are used to living under hygienic conditions. And you get food so rarely that you throw yourself over it. Most things are arranged so that you will behave like an animal. (Latin America)

The Hungarian exiled philosopher Heller (1985) has analysed the *power of shame*. She considers shame to be the very emotion that makes us adjust to our cultural environment. Shame is universally the first and basic moral feeling, and internalized by the child at a very early stage: 'When the child learns of what he or she should be ashamed, he or she learns thereby the legitimization of a system of domination' (Ibid. p. 40). The external power is internalized in the feeling of shame. This is society's silent voice, or 'the eye of others' that we hear and sense inside us: 'It makes us blush and hide our faces; it arouses the desire to run away, to sink into the earth, to disappear'

(Ibid. p. 5). And the prostitute, Heller says, is the symbol of shame. She is the 'embodiment of lost honour' (Ibid. p. 56). To turn the woman into a whore is thus the pervasive and fundamental goal of torture.

> I think that many men who torture a politically active woman try to convince themselves that she is a kind of whore. They know, too, that many of us were much more liberated than other women. I think it was easier for them to torture a woman who was a whore than a woman who could be like their own mothers or daughters. There has to be a kind of separation: "I can act like this toward this woman because she is not like my mother or my wife or my daughter." There must be a lot of prejudice against us political women. But our lives were also very different from the traditional woman's. I think there are many men who don't think politics is anything for women. (Latin America)

Inside The Cell, women are shown that those who dare to enter male territory become 'public women'. It is as if these 'public women' can be deprived of their public, *political* visibility only by removing them from the public space and forcing public *sexual* visibility upon them, inside the private space of The Cell. By inducing shame through this contamination, those in power seek to deprive them of their social and political power – because the power of shame is overwhelming.

> Then, I was very, very thin, and I didn't have large breasts. Of course, they try to humiliate you, but in a way I was glad that I wasn't very attractive, that I didn't have a very feminine shape. But they laughed a lot and said: "Ha, you don't have any breasts." Or: 'what a body you have." And being in a room without knowing how many men were around you when you have a blindfold on and are completely naked. . . . It was a strange feeling. It's hard to – you simply feel so exposed when you are naked. (Latin America)

In the political technology of torture of the female body all available methods are employed to induce a sense of contamination. Naturally, menstrual blood, which symbolizes both something pure and beautiful and something impure and shameful, is a suitable instrument. Through this symbolic attitude toward her blood, a woman's ambiguity is threatened: she is no longer both madonna and whore; she is now only a whore. 'Then I got my menstruation, and I didn't have anything to use. They didn't care whether you had menstruation or not. Finally, a young soldier came with some rags and said: "can you use these?"' (Latin America)

In torture's political technology of the female body, masculine forms of power are crystallized into premeditated patterns which are everywhere

where torture is practised. A representative of the exile Iraqi women's organization, Dr Su'ad Khairi (1982, p. 31) says about prison:

> They are animals that enjoy torturing women. When they receive young women prisoners, they begin by making cheap offers, and then they strip them and give them electric shocks on the most sensitive parts of the body. They throw the victim on the floor and threaten to rape her and take nude pictures of her which they will publish or send to her family.

The shame inherent inside the private space of The Cell is reinforced through the media. Those who see such pictures cannot know whether or not the women have given their consent. Suspicion of complicity can be sufficient to generate social contamination and shame.

> If the police had arrested me, I would have been raped. I knew that some of my comrades had been raped in prison. Ten or twenty policemen came at once. When they left the prison, they were completely. . . . Therefore, my family and I were very frightened. That was why they helped me get out of the country. (Middle East)

Contamination disgraces the woman, and also – especially – the men in her family. She can therefore risk being expelled by her own people after she is released. Thus, the ring is closed and those in power have attained their highest goal: to function as quietly as possible by making the people themselves the origin of their own repression. 'When I was released, I had to swear that they had not hurt me. "Isn't that right?" they asked. "Yes," I said. *"Be careful*," they said to me.' (Latin America)

5. The Mother's Room

The children have been a grounding for me. If I hadn't had my child in my homeland, I would have burned out like a flame – without a doubt. I am completely happy in my children. I do not regret having always been alone with them. It hasn't been easy, but I cannot remember a single moment of my life when I have regretted having them. (Latin America)

So far, we have been concerned with the individual girl or woman as part of the system of power in the homeland. We have heard stories from The Daughter's Room and The Father's Room, and from the streets and secret cells of the dictatorship. And we have heard the individual woman's story of her life in and against the system. We have been especially interested in the social control of the woman's body, symbolized both in the relationship to blood and to the transgression of sexual boundaries. And we have heard the story of the strategies carried out by those with political power to discipline and punish dangerous women. We understand them to be sexually disgracing strategies for the purpose of divesting the woman of political power. In these stories, we have heard the individual woman's reflections about these experiences and about her 'self'. But the stories have unavoidably been populated with many other people important to her. Her experiences have meant something for her relationships to the important people in the close family system. Through her relationships to these people, she has experienced herself and the consequences of the violence she was subject to.

We have now left the darkness of The Cell and entered a new room: the space which is defined by the woman's relationship to the child and to herself as mother. In the male-dominated society, the woman must be careful that others do not transgress her boundaries; she must be careful when she enters male territory; but there is also something more she must be careful of. In the midst of rebellion and violence, she must be careful of her children – both the unborn child she carries in her body, and the children she takes with her in flight and into exile.

Care of children is closely connected to the feminine space and to its position outside the public area. The asymmetric sexual division of labour, which makes the woman especially responsible for the 'private' labour of caring for the home and giving and nurturing life, creates special female priorities (Brun 1991). These priorities are a fundamental part of the historically transmitted patterns of meaning and inevitably influence her relationship to herself and to the system of which she is a part.

How is this 'self' the women have reflected about related to the children and to the larger system of power? According to Bateson (1972, pp. 331–32), the self as we understand it is 'only a little part of a much larger trial-and-error system which thinks, acts, decides. . . . The self is a false objectification of an incorrectly defined part of a much larger complex of processes that work together'. The whole think-and-act system made up of the woman and her children is influenced by the power strategies of the dictatorship, and she can encounter severe conflict with her female priorities when she chooses to transgress the boundaries of the system. In the short-term, these priorities perhaps mean that she must remain in the private sphere and care for her children, but seen in a longer perspective, the political struggle against the dictatorship in the public sphere is perhaps the best care she can give her children.

Bateson apparently has these female priorities and their inherent conflicts in mind when he attempts to understand concepts such as 'self' and 'power'. Unlike Foucault, he does not see human beings' oppression as a kind of fate that is almost structurally integrated within the conditions of life. Maybe there exists a more life-giving path, a path that offers the possibility of an existence of greater freedom, provided we understand how to live in harmony with the larger system of which we are part: the larger system which is a part of all life on earth. In order to find the connection to this larger system, however, it is necessary to see 'one's self' as part of this whole, which consists not only of social, political and cultural systems but ecological ones, too. A human being is also a biological being that must survive in nature. 'If the being destroys its environment, it also destroys itself' (Bateson 1972, p. 332), and here Bateson understands environment in its broadest sense. Wrong or even catastrophic reactions can occur, if we do not live in harmony with this larger pattern.

The dictatorship is an example of such a wrong and catastrophic connection between human beings and the system to which they belong. It is a connection that threatens the woman's relationship to the child *inside* her body, waiting to be born; and it is a connection which threatens the relationship to the child who has left her body and lives *outside* as an independent being: the power of the dictatorship once more becomes visible in the conflict she can experience in her common life with the child during flight and exile.

Inside the space of the body

Giving birth exceeded all my expectations. I had never imagined it could be so exciting. It is the most exciting thing I have ever experienced in my life. It is something that . . . I don't have the words to describe it. It is simply *life*. When I saw the baby for the first time, it was as if – oh, I don't know – life, life – I can produce life! (Latin America)

Something in this relationship is fundamentally different from the power myth of the dictatorship. In the concern for and the idea of new life, which pregnancy represents, the child in the womb is actual new life. It also represents The New Life, The New World. The woman is giving life to a new human being, but she will thereby also contribute to creation of the world.

I had my child because I lived in the mountains, and there was no place you could get an abortion. The first three or four months I really hated myself – it depends of course on how the relationship is between the woman and the man. But after I felt the baby's first movements, something great happened. I thought about the other life inside me, and I loved it so much and took care of it. I stopped thinking about my husband. He was something outside, and he had only done it for two minutes. I felt that it was *my* child. (Middle East)

But the little private system consisting of mother and child is a lonely system in the midst of a world dominated by violence. The child becomes both her strength and her weakness.

I gave birth to my first child in a strange city during flight. I didn't cry or scream like the other women on the ward. They all screamed and swore, but I kept it all inside me. But when the baby was born, I cried – after it was all over. The doctor was surprised and asked: "Why are you crying? They tell me you were such a quiet woman who didn't scream. Why are you crying now, when it doesn't hurt any more?" I didn't know. Today, I don't know either. I didn't cry out of happiness. I think it was a sense of loneliness that I still feel. (Middle East)

The mother–child system is vulnerable in the midst of this world, if it isn't surrounded by a protective shield. This protection can consist of an inner shield that the mother might be able to establish, but usually it is the task of the father to ensure this protection. If no such protection exists, the strength of the mother–child relationship can turn into weakness and loneliness, and the selves of both the mother and the child can be threatened or injured (Winnicott 1986).

My first birth was difficult. It took one and a half days and it was at a hospital. My mother, my sister and my husband's mother were with me. We didn't have any preparation for giving birth as you do in Denmark, so I had only heard about it from my mother and my sister. But five days after giving birth, my husband had to flee to a neighbouring country; the police were after him because of his political activities. I was very sad about it. It was also strange for me to be a mother. Many times I sat beside my son and looked at his face and thought: "is it true that this is my baby?" I don't know why, but before I felt very strong; but after I had my son, I sometimes felt so weak. (Middle East)

A baby brings a new vulnerability in relation to the dictatorship, but the mother may choose to give the resistance struggle first priority so that finally they both can survive. However, the loss of the child in the service of a greater cause is experienced as lasting pain and a terrible conflict:

I left my son, but my sister is with him. You know, my situation is special, and the situation in my country is very strange. Maybe there are some people who speak badly of me, because I left my little baby with my family. But my whole family is politically active, so it is not strange for them. And they forbade me to take my baby with me. They said: "if you die, you have chosen it yourself. But if they catch you and kill your child, who is responsible? And who has allowed you to do that to him?" Maybe he will choose a completely different ideology when he is grown-up. So I couldn't take him with me. It was very hard for me to leave him. I am really so sorry that I did it. It is actually my biggest problem.

I stayed up in the mountains for four years; then we fled to a neighbouring country, and then to another before we came to Denmark. I haven't seen my son since he was a year old. He is eight now, so it is a very long time not to see him. In the beginning, I couldn't get any news of him, because it was difficult to send and receive letters in the mountains. But since we came to Denmark, we call him on the telephone. I remember the first time I spoke to my little son and my two sisters. We spoke for more than 45 minutes.

At the time I left him, I didn't think it was so important even if I was away for ten years – if only I could do something good for my country. But we didn't succeed. I believed in the theory, but not in the way they put it into practice. The leaders had the wrong ideology. But it was hard for me to leave my child, and before I had my new child, it was very hard. Now it is a little better – maybe because I have heard how he is and we talk together sometimes. He is well, because my sister loves him very much. He lives well now, because my sister has work and she has no children of her own. She takes good care of him. But it is impossible to bring him to Denmark, because if I apply for him to leave the country maybe they will kill him. It is very hard. For example, I knew a woman – she was my friend. She had a six-month-old baby, and they tortured the baby with electricity. He died of it. It was terrible. So I will not speak to my government about my little child, because I want him to be safe. But it is hard for me to live so far away from him. (Middle East)

This vulnerability of the mother–child system is exploited by those in power in their sexual–political strategy toward the female body:

I really believed I would give birth to a monster. The whole time I was in prison, I was pregnant. That means that he was tortured with me. I thought he would be an over-hysterical baby when he was born – or he would be sick. He was sick, too, when he was born. He had a cyst in his middle ear that affected his throat so he couldn't eat. I gave him food with a spoon. Fortunately, he's more or less normal. I have talked with him about all the things that happened. I still think that it must have affected him in some way, and that it must come out at some point. I was given electric shock many times while I was three, four months pregnant. There was also the psychological pressure all the time. It must have affected him. At some time or other something will happen, don't you think? (Latin America)

Those in power, with their disciplinary and punitive invasion of her body, have found her most vulnerable area. By striking the body, they strike the soul, and their attack becomes lodged inside her as a lasting anxiety that the child will be 'wrong'. Contamination can infect the child who is a part of her. The impurity they seek to inflict on her can be transferred to the unborn child, who loses his humanity and becomes a 'monster'. They try to kill the child inside her both physically and psychologically.

The birth process itself is threatened by the dictatorship system. The muscles tighten with anxiety when you live illegally and fear apprehension every moment:

My husband wouldn't go to prison, so we lived illegally at first. But after a while, it was almost impossible to live that way. We had false names, and we lived in different places. Sometimes we stayed in one room without going outside for a whole month, and friends came with food for us. There was strong military pressure then, and many were imprisoned and tortured. So we fled from place to place. Finally, we fled to a little island, where we pretended we were newly married and that my husband was an artist. We said we had fled from our families. We hoped to live in safety on that island, but it became difficult when I became pregnant. We wanted to have the baby, but it was terrible to experience that in that place. I can't bear to remember it. I couldn't go to the hospital to be examined, because I had a false name and identity card. But when I went into labour, I had to go to the hospital. There was no ferry, and the naval station on the island had the only boat. The crossing took a long time and I felt terrible. My waters broke during the trip. When I arrived at the hospital, there was no medicine for the pain. I was so far along that they didn't ask me about anything but just helped me deliver. I was in the hospital for two or three days, and I was constantly afraid that the police would come if they found out who I was. I was also afraid during delivery. If you are afraid, you tense your muscles and the labour stops. So after the waters broke, the baby wouldn't come out and it was very painful. An old doctor helped me. He was kind – he was just like my father. My husband gave him a gift, and he didn't ask much about who we were.

I returned to our little island, and we were completely alone. I couldn't tell anyone about the baby, not my own family or my husband's. There was no one to help us so we had to take care of everything ourselves. We didn't have much money. Before, we had lived well – we both had good education and good jobs. It became so hard that finally my husband couldn't stand living there. He left. He went to Denmark on a false passport. I stayed on the island with my three-month-old baby boy. I stayed there for six more months, until winter, and then I needed many things for the baby so I decided to return to my family. They didn't know what had happened, that I was married and had a child. They only knew that I had some political problems. We hid in my mother's house and never went out. We had a room, and if guests came, we had to hide; I gave my son chocolate so he wouldn't cry. No one knew that I had a son or anything about my problems. But time went by and I couldn't do anything or plan anything for the future. I didn't want to leave the country with a little baby. I kept waiting for the situation in my country to change so my husband could come home again. But time went by and there were more and more problems in the country. We read and heard about how many died under torture. Finally, I didn't dare stay. It was very hard to stay inside for such a long time. During all those months, I was only outside once to visit my sister, after dark. I took good care of the baby, but he got fat. He had no room to play and he became unhealthy. (Middle East)

The little system consisting of the mother and the foetus are part of a larger system that threatens its survival. It is as if the body will not let go of the baby but will keep it inside its protective room:

During my first birth, I had problems. It didn't progress as it should, and he was taken with forceps. Also, all the afterbirth wasn't expelled. You had to be careful, and I was scared to take medicine for fear of saying something that was forbidden. And when they asked: "Where is your husband?" What should I say? I don't like to lie, so sometimes I told them – it could have had bad consequences to tell that he was in prison. But I didn't feel it was anything to be ashamed of. They should know that there were some political prisoners. Some reacted negatively – were afraid. Maybe that's why I had those problems with the delivery. It was also because we couldn't write to each other, and he was in prison far from where I lived. So I waited and waited, and I knew I was going to give birth. I wanted a letter before I went to the hospital, but none came. So I thought about it all the time. He was in prison, so I thought about how it was there – whether he got any food. I think that's why the birth wasn't normal. (Latin America)

Pregnancy is not a happy experience. The surroundings are strange and cold. The important source of information – the mothers and sisters belonging to the woman's family – is not available. There is no protective female space around her. But when she sees her baby, she can recognize and recreate that space out of her joy for the baby:

I wanted to have an abortion, but my sister wrote to me that maybe I could never be pregnant again if I got an abortion the first time I was pregnant. So I agreed to have the baby even though I didn't really want it. I wasn't happy about having the baby, and I was angry with myself for getting pregnant, because I knew what to do to avoid it. My girl friend had taught me the calendar method, but I got pregnant the first month after we were married. It was hard giving birth to her. When I went into labour, I was alone in the dormitory. The waters broke and I didn't know what it was. I just felt as if I had to go to the toilet, and I felt the pains – but what should I do? I had heard that women should walk in that situation, so I went back and forth in the corridor. I couldn't eat and I couldn't sleep. There was just the pain and I was frightened. I felt very alone. Finally, I went to someone from my country whose room was on the same corridor and she contacted a doctor who called an ambulance. It took two days and I was alone in the hospital. It wasn't like in Denmark, where the husband is allowed to be there. In my country, your mother and sister are usually there. But there, in a transit country, you are just alone, and they couldn't explain anything to me because I couldn't understand a word of their language. But when I saw the baby, I felt it was I who had created her. She was a part of my body. I was very happy. Now I knew why my mother had loved us and lived her whole life to make us happy. Now I am very happy I have a child. She is seven, and I will teach her everything I have learned from my life. (Middle East)

To have a child is a critical event in any family system. The baby's arrival radically changes the relationships between the family members, and this change is normally associated with stress arising from the effort to find a new balance. This new balance must be established both between the individual and the family system and between the family and the surrounding society. A normal event such as the birth of a child is also one which creates crisis, and it will reinforce the problems the family might already have (McCubbin & McCubbin 1989).

When the birth of a child occurs during flight or in exile, the family is almost bombarded with demands to change its structure. You are forced to try to find a new balance as well as you can:

The birth – it happened without my understanding a word of Danish. I arrived at the hospital at night with my sweetheart, and we were left alone in a big room. He spoke with them – a little in English and a little in Danish. I understood a little English. The personnel just left me there. I had never seen such a delivery room before. I didn't know anything about what it was used for, and I didn't know what was supposed to happen. I had been to the doctor, and it was just like with the Pakistani women today. I just sat there and they talked over my head. I didn't understand very much and they didn't care. I didn't feel they treated me right. People were unbelievably cold and indifferent. There weren't so many foreigners in Denmark then. Now after 15 years I can feel the difference. Denmark was completely different then.

I was in an old-fashioned hospital, and I lay there all night and didn't dilate very much. In the morning, I was given intravenous medicine to stimulate labour, but they didn't tell me anything. It's also all those prejudices. They think you are dumb because you come from a Third World country. They told me it was to make me feel better. I didn't know what it was, but I had a normal delivery about five in the afternoon. Afterwards, I slept for 24 hours – I was really worn out. I was in the hospital for five days and had to get by with sign language. The baby was put beside my bed, and I didn't know anything about what I should do.

I felt that it was my baby, and it was a beautiful baby. It wasn't me but another human being whom I should learn to love. But I had a strange feeling of emptiness: "Oh, now I had a baby, and it was my baby," I said that to myself many times. I didn't love the baby right away. It came after a while. Before the baby had been inside me, and now it was outside, and it was a stranger whom I had to get to know. This feeling of separation was very strong. Suddenly it wasn't inside me; it was another human being.

So I just stayed home and took care of the baby and was alone and isolated again. And I kept losing weight. I was with the baby all the time and changed it every hour or hour and a half. And I nursed it – at night, I nursed six or seven times. We lived in a very poor apartment where it was cold during the winter. It was heated with a kerosene stove – it was out of order and we couldn't get it to work. I had never seen such a heater before. And it smelled. The visiting nurse said it was unhealthy. I felt we lived a very poor life then and it made me very upset. I had never lived so poorly before. It wasn't normal for me, but it was poverty: a bad apartment, loose windows. Everything was old. The floor was cold. And I did everything instinctively – put an electric heater in his bedroom because the other heater was unhealthy for him. I tried to protect the baby – have a little colour. I never slept. I never really got dressed – went around in my bathrobe all the time because I could never get anything done. I was with the baby all the time. I never went out on the street. My sweetheart did the shopping. I never saw anyone, a car, the sun, anything. For three months I was just in the apartment. Then the visiting nurse said I should stop nursing, and when I gave him a bottle, he slept through the night for the first time. After that it went better, and we also moved to a better apartment. It was in the suburbs. It was a terrible neighbourhood. I became even more isolated. (Latin America)

When a baby is born at the beginning of exile, several crushing problems arise simultaneously, and the actual survival of the mother–child system becomes the dominant problem. An attempt is therefore made to shut out the surroundings which are strange and feel threatening, either by physical isolation or by denying their existence. All available attention and energy must be focused on the survival of the mother–child relationship. This can cause a polarizing of the roles in the family. In this situation, the father must provide the connections to the outside world, but his protection against the threatening world can also become too inflexible. A self-reinforcing process begins which can escalate so that the father becomes more and more involved outside the home and the mother becomes even more isolated. This polarization of roles can break the relationship apart (Sluzki 1979). Life as a single mother can become reality in the women's house of exile.

Outside the space of the body

But to be a mother – that's really me. It is the best experience. I wouldn't have missed it for anything. That's where I get my strength and everything that is good. And my children – they really love me so very much. They have a very close relationship to me. The two oldest can talk to me about everything, and they support me, and I support them. (Latin America)

In exile, children can be a source of both strength and weakness. When the child has been separated from the woman's body and become a 'stranger' that moves about outside in the public space, it will react independently to the power of the dictatorship and to flight and exile. Many children arrive with their own traumatic experiences in addition to experiencing a period full of crisis for their parents.

> My boy has many psychological problems. He is lonely and won't go outside to play. He keeps asking about the police and the soldiers and is afraid they will capture his father. I think it is because of those years when we had to stay inside our room. Sometimes I am afraid that it will continue all his life. I think my husband should help the boy. In a way, it is his fault we are here, even though I don't want to think in that way. But the contact between the two of them is not very good. (Middle East)

Like all other families that experience changes within their system or in the environment, refugee families also react differently. The Latin American exile psychiatrist Carlos Sluzki (1979) tries, however, to outline a basic pattern for the various phases of reaction. If he were to make a graphic representation of the process undergone by a family as it passes through these phases, it would resemble one of the well-known graphs from the psychology of performance under stress. During the preparation and flight phase itself, the family performs pretty well, while during the phase just after arrival, there is a strong rise in its performance and feeling of well-being – happiness and surprise at having arrived safely. 'The best about Denmark is that there is peace. We can sleep all night, and my children aren't afraid. I am happy here because of my children.' (Middle East)

In the next phase of crisis, the graph shows a sharp decline, and it takes several years to climb back to the level reached just before flight. The graph then finally levels out into the phase of the next generation. Each phase has its specific characteristics which cause various reactions from the family, and these in turn, in a chain reaction, cause various conflicts and symptoms.

> My son began in nursery school right away. Now, I think it was stupid of me to let him go from me right away, because he didn't know anyone. He didn't know the language. I just let him go and went to language school myself. I lost a lot by doing that. He didn't say a word until two years ago, either in our own language or in Danish. He didn't speak at all and he was unhappy. He didn't want to go to nursery school. He cried and wanted to stay with me. But he started to talk in kindergarten. He missed his grandparents and said: "Grandma is coming to get me." (Middle East)

Whose fault is exile? It is easy to privatize the common political problem. The mother has to try to establish contact with the new public space, at the same time as she must care for her child, who has his own trauma to struggle with. Forced separation from parents during flight, for example, leaves the child with feelings of anxiety and frightening memories which return in the form of nightmares:

> When we fled up into the mountains, my youngest child was only two months and my oldest two years old. We left them with my husband's family and lived in the mountains for a year. Then we disagreed with our group and had to flee from there. We didn't have time to tell the family that we had to leave. We sent a letter and then rode on horse-back across the border. Almost two years later, I was able to go from Denmark and fetch them. I travelled to the border area where there was war and contacted some people and paid them a lot of money. They know all the secrets and have some methods we don't know about. I don't know them – nobody knows them. But they got my children for me. Now I try to make the children feel secure, and I won't leave them again. But they are insecure, because for example when we passed by some guards, they shot at us. That is a frightening experience for a four-year-old child. Now I have problems with my oldest son. He screams and cries at night, and I forget about my own problems when I see him. He is so little. (Middle East)

When the family system breaks down during the phase of crisis in exile, the woman has to try to establish a life as a single mother and a new relationship to her child's father. There are no traditions in life in the Middle Eastern homeland on which to base such a new relationship. For the man, life as a Scandinavian 'divorced father', which requires him to give up his demands on his wife, is very difficult to accept:

> I am not happy with my life. And she [my daughter] notices it if I am even just a little mad or cry. Then she gets angry with me, because she loves me. She has only had me for these seven years. She has never felt that she had a father. I want to give her everything. But sometimes I feel sorry for her, because I haven't been able to give her a father's care – couldn't be a father and mother at the same time. But she is happy to live with me. She doesn't want to live with her father. If I tell her she is to be with him, she cries and says it is my fault her father came to Denmark. She feels divided between her father and me, because he pumps her for information all the time about my life and my boyfriend.
>
> I haven't felt happy for ten years, and now I think that it will never be any better. If my ex-husband lives in Denmark, he will always keep

bothering me. That means I'll never be free. Political freedom – we don't have that in my country. And inside myself – in my life – I don't have any freedom either. I don't feel like we have a home here in Denmark. I am still a foreigner here; and I don't have my family; I don't have my country. I am unhappy all the time. (Middle East)

Even though change is experienced as impossible, family systems – just like other systems – are in a constant process of change; they only seem to be stable. This also applies to the little mother–child system or the father–mother–children system. This is an important starting point, if one wishes to help a family therapeutically: if the family is considered a fixed, unchanging system, the therapist's strategy would be to 'correct the mistake'. Conversely, if the family is seen as a system in a continuous process of development and only *seems* stable, the therapist's job is to ease the natural development process (Marner 1987). The words 'never' and 'always' could, in the story we have just heard, be replaced with 'once' and 'just now'.

I come from a large city where women work just like men. Therefore, women decide more in my home town. It's not like in the country or in the mountains, where the man decides. It's going to be like that for my daughter, too. If she says, "Mother, I want to marry," then I will say: "yes, that's for you to decide for yourself." I will never forget how it was when I got married. I love my daughter very much, so I will let her decide, also if she wishes to marry a Dane. It is she, and not I, who is to be married. My daughter is very pretty and she is clever in school. She is in the tenth grade, and I think she wants to go to the gymnasium afterwards. She speaks fluent Danish – not like me. I didn't go to language school very long. I stayed home and thought about my family in my homeland. (Middle East)

The daughter is a source of strength during the exile crisis of the mother, who, although plagued by the loss of her homeland, can still find something positive in the marginality of her new life.

The degree of conflict and symptoms in the next generation also depends on the parent generation's ability to meet the demands of the first phases of the exile process. 'Everything the first generation has avoided will show up in the second generation – usually as a conflict between the generations' (Sluzki 1979, p. 387). The meeting with the public space of exile is unavoidable, and the mother can either accept or reject that reality. The worry of the next mother (as well as her not worrying) probably also contains an unconscious recognition that systems change in their unavoidable relationship with their surroundings. If she remains in exile too long, she might experience a split between herself and her daughters:

I'm not worried that my daughters will be influenced by Danish morals. When they came here they were 20 or 23 and they were "well built" inside. They don't want to be like Danish girls – with sexual freedom. They want to marry, and it has to be with a man from our country. It's hard to find one here, because all our men want to live with Danish girl-friends. It's easier for the men. That's a problem. I hope we can return soon, because I'm worried about my daughters. (Middle East)

The rebellion of puberty is reinforced by the split that exile can cause between the generations. The reaction to the daughter's rebellion against the refugee's marginal position is full of conflict – because there is always a feeling of being to blame for the daughter's problems: it isn't her fault that she is in exile. The feeling of blame makes it difficult to set limits for the daughter:

My oldest daughter started to live rather wildly, according to our way of thinking, when she was 15 or 16. She only had Danish friends – and we didn't think anything could happen if she stayed overnight at their homes. I was actually permissive. But she started doing badly in school. That was difficult for me to accept. I saw it was having a bad effect on her. I saw it happening during all these years; I saw that things weren't going better for her. So when she was in the ninth grade, I told her that I would not accept that she smoked hash. She answered that she didn't care and then she moved out to live with some girl-friends. She rebelled strongly – especially against me. We had a very bad relationship. I had an idea that we had been very flexible with them, and young people have to rebel. So she had to find something that would hurt us – something that would frighten us. That's what it was. And when we reacted as we did, we kept her in that situation. But we couldn't do anything else. I have thought about it a lot, but I can't accept it. I must accept the fact that she is a very irresponsible girl. I care for her very much, but I have to acknowledge how immature she is. Now it is four or five years since she moved, but she still comes home every day – and I'm glad she does – she comes to eat breakfast, wash clothes, take a bath, eat dinner. That means that she wants to decide what she does in her free time for herself, while in all other respects she acts like a child from our country. It's a double moral standard, but I accept it. What else can I do? But I feel she exploits the situation that she is both from our country and is Danish. It is very typical for our country that we don't throw our children out. We don't disown them. She has the key to our apartment, and everything that belongs to us also belongs to our children. That is typically Latin American. In a way there are permanent ties in the Latin American family and I am very happy about that. But in return the family has a certain right to be involved in the lives of its members. Also when they marry. We don't have this right here, because our children are Danish. That is not good for us.

I can see that my oldest daughter has lost some values along the way. That's how I see it. That's why I think it is a shame that she is here. But she doesn't know anything else now. I think all her problems are caused by our life in exile, and are also connected to the time when she was four and her father was away for a long time; and she lost him psychologically once more when we came to Denmark. That was a defeat for my husband. He was unhappy and developed a stomach ulcer. He couldn't be useful in Denmark. So he lost something of himself, and she experienced that.

It also has to do with her hearing that foreigners are not welcome in Denmark. She is on the defensive. I think she has a conflict with our way of raising our children because she must be more Danish than the Danes themselves. She has to be in the forefront of rebellion. She must in any case not be a girl from a Catholic country, because she has heard about "the oppressed women in Latin America" and "the women in Catholic countries". I don't think that is the right way to formulate the problem. I formulate it for myself this way: when I came to Denmark, I had my identity, so I didn't doubt myself or my background. But she had no secure background, so it was enormously difficult for her to find her identity. Who is she? And what is her background? In the beginning she was one of us, because she was loyal to us. But later, she rebelled against us. She wants to be Danish. She's a lovely girl, but she is not Danish. And she knows that, too. But I am very much in doubt about what I should do to help her. She is most important to my life. I am very much in doubt. I have never tried it before, to be a parent and in exile. (Latin America)

The daughter has been the victim of a double 'father loss', and after all these years, the father still remains in the crisis phase and suffers from psychosomatic symptoms. The girl reproduces the parents' ambiguous feelings toward the homeland, which is simultaneously both idealized and denigrated.

We were also stupid. The children always had to be with us when they were little, at all our meetings, solidarity arrangements etc. We didn't have any family who could care for them while we were out. We were both active in political work. So the children saw films about torture and they heard about it. They were tired of it. What kind of picture did they get of their parents' homeland? They couldn't identify with it.

They became Danish children with Danish values and friends, sweethearts and school. They talk about visiting our country to see how it is. But they have an idea of it which does not compare to reality. So I think it will be difficult for them, if they should live there for example. On the other hand, I also have an idea that maybe they could find happiness there. I don't think they are especially happy here. But if they stay here, then I will also stay, because I can't leave my children. For the time being, we are here, but we are very divided. (Latin America)

The idea of the homeland is very significant for how the family deals with the crisis phase. Some families succeed in living through a period of mourning during which they say farewell to the old country, and, through a constructive process, unite the old rules, models and habits with the new reality. In other families, the homeland becomes increasingly idealized while the new country is denigrated; this of course complicates life in exile. Still other families experience a process which is just the opposite. The homeland is increasingly denigrated or denied and the new country idealized. This complicates the process of mourning and of coming to terms with their loss (Sluzki 1979).

But as we heard in the last story, refugee life as a whole is also a story of division. You cannot say farewell to the old country without betraying your struggle: exile is an act of aggression and saying farewell to the old country can be experienced as surrender to the power of the dictatorship. The homeland as a whole, though, can be neither denigrated nor idealized. Some aspects of the homeland are condemnable: those aspects represented by the dictatorship; but some are idealized: the land you have struggled to liberate.

I have paid for it with my two children. I have lost my two children. I mean that is not anything I am especially proud of. We had to try to survive – that has been the theme of our life together, my children and I. And I was able to survive because I was an adult. I am strong. But my children – they were little and they weren't strong. And there were really a lot of things they couldn't understand. It was terribly hard for them – all the things I've been through. It wasn't only my own past and my adjustment to Danish ways, but also our family, which is a part of the past, and our social customs. All that was smashed. It has really cost me so much, and it isn't anything I can brag about. My daughter has serious psychological problems because when she was little she always lived in a state of insecurity and anxiety. The worst was that we never had a permanent place to live; we moved from one place to another. That also meant that the children had to change schools and move from one country to another. When they came to Denmark, they already spoke two languages: Spanish and Portuguese, and now they had to learn a third.

Our first meeting with the Danish society was very violent. The

children had problems in school, where there were many other refugee
children. They were in fights almost every day, and one day my daughter
came home with two broken fingers, because a teacher had slammed a
door on them. The other children also hit my son. There was violence,
violence – all the time. And there wasn't a single day when the children
didn't come home without bruises. There were also problems among the
refugees here in Denmark. We belonged to different political groups and
parties, and we couldn't even agree. Everyone talked about the others
behind their backs, and all that kind of thing. That really bothered me,
because I thought we would find peace here, but we only found another
battlefield. It has been especially hard on my daughter. My son is more
goal-oriented. He wished to learn and adjust as quickly as he could, and
he did that. But my daughter is more split. It is hard for her to play with
the other children. She simply could not make contact with them, partly
because we had lived in such isolation so long. And the children also had
a bad relationship with each other. They have always been like that, and I
never had any help to deal with it.

My daughter has been expelled from all the foster homes, schools and
institutions she has been sent to. That's also because she got mixed up in
drug abuse and some criminality and all that. She is 15 now. She sleeps
during the day and goes out at night. Sometimes she sleeps for several
days. She is a difficult girl. She has always been difficult, and it's not hard
to understand why. But they are going to find out what's best for her. The
welfare office takes care of her. The social workers, psychologists etc.,
have all advised me not to even dream about getting her back. She has
also tried to commit suicide. So I don't feel very good about her, because
I don't know what to do. I have my life – now she has to find hers. (Latin
America)

In their life in exile, children may have to suffer symptoms caused by the
abuse carried out by those in power in the homeland. The mother's feeling of
being to blame for these symptoms causes an unbearable conflict inside her.
The only solution is for her to accept the split between her and her children.
This next mother tries to hold on to the connection between the private and
political perspectives, to protect herself from feeling complicit:

My son doesn't do anything. He smokes hash and is greatly depressed.
He also fights with his girl-friend a lot. Then she comes and lives with me,
because my son would beat her. I defend her, and then my son turns
against me. He doesn't work. He doesn't study. He smokes ten grams of
hash a day. Where does he get the money to smoke? By stealing. But I
don't think it's the fault of Danish society. The military is to blame. It
was the military that split our family. It is their fault that I came to

Denmark, and it is their fault that my son and daughter don't have any
education. Because in my country, family life is completely different. My
son was separated from his grandparents whom he loved dearly. And
when I came here, I started working hard. Not because anyone said I
should work – I wanted to. So I sent my children to nursery school at six in
the morning, and when they came home at five in the afternoon, I made
dinner. I was so tired. It was one big mess. Do you understand? But I
don't say that it is the fault of Danish society. In no way. I respect this
society. I love Denmark as my own country. (Latin America)

In the strained situation of the family in exile, ill-defined boundaries can
emerge between the generations: children come to function as parents; roles
are exchanged, either because the parents are not able to fulfil their care-
taking functions, or maybe because the children feel responsible for the
family's problems – 'The child becomes a parent for its parents, and thereby
also a parent for itself' (Bustos & Ruggiero 1986, p. 14). The children take
over the feeling of complicity. As children, it is impossible for them to
understand private suffering in a political context.

My oldest daughter was two when we came to Denmark. She was afraid
all the time when she was a child. She was afraid of strangers, and she was
afraid of men. She wouldn't let go of me, and when I was going to leave
the room to go out and make food for her, she would scream. She always
held on to me. I think it was because I failed her while my husband was in
prison. I had to work then, and I didn't have anyone to take care of her,
so I left her with my aunt. It was just at the time when she started to walk
and talk. But I had no choice. I didn't have any money either, so I
couldn't go home and visit her. When I finally went to get her, she was
very distant and aggressive the first few days. But gradually it passed. It is
possible that some of that still sits inside her, because she was very sad
during the first years we lived here. She never wanted to go down and
play. While she grew up, she was always alone without any girl-friends.
Now she has several, but she didn't play much during her childhood.
She's a very sensible girl today, but it's as if she always wants to take care
of me. She always tries to take over her father's role when he's not there.
There must be some things that have affected her. (Latin America)

The child's experience of its parents being mistreated by authority figures
such as the police, or being arrested and imprisoned, can destroy the picture
of its parents as strong and invincible protectors. The parents are exposed in
all their vulnerability, and the child dare not express its anxiety to them, but
must instead take over the function of taking care of them. The dynamics of
this situation also include that form of 'magic thinking' which is common

among little children. They cannot differentiate between fantasy and reality and believe that their aggressive and destructive fantasies can cause external events. They can therefore believe that the misfortune that strikes their parents or their family is caused by their bad behaviour or 'evil' feelings toward their parents (Carli 1987). The child's feeling of complicity can be concealed as a shameful secret that is first revealed to the mother by accident, as in this story about ice-cream:

My son was seven years old then, and one morning he went out on the street to play. He met another boy, our neighbour's son, who was supposed to go to the store to buy milk and bread. My son offered to sell him a little drawing, and the other boy bought it for the money he should have used to buy milk and bread. My son used the money to buy some ice-cream, but the other boy's mother got very angry about it. I don't really understand why, because it wasn't very much money. My son came home and said: "Mother, mother, that lady says she will call the police if I don't give her the money back." I said, "you'll have to solve that yourself. I can't give you the money." That was a big mistake. But my son went to the man that sold him the ice-cream and wanted him to give back the money, but of course he wouldn't. Just that day the police came to arrest me – just as my son came back to the house. The police were all over the neighbourhood, and he thought it was *his* fault I was arrested. But of course it wasn't. He watched while they arrested me and led me out to the police car. And when they drove away, he began to vomit.

Several years later, after we came to Denmark, my daughter asked me why I had been arrested. My son answered: "It was my fault." I said: "No, it wasn't your fault. You were too little – you weren't involved in anything political." And he again told the story about the ice cream. I said: "You must absolutely not believe that it was your fault. One of my comrades betrayed me." Then I called Germany, where that comrade is in exile, and I told him to tell my son that it was he who had sent the police to our house and that it wasn't my son. "I can't do that," he said, but I told him that I didn't care and that I would take my son to Germany so he could tell him the truth if he refused to do it on the telephone. So he told my son everything. He explained to him why he had betrayed me, and my son relaxed. But for all those years, he had believed that it was his fault that his mother was put in prison. (Latin America)

We have listened to some mothers' stories. They took place within the definitional space which we have called The Mother's Room – these are *their* stories. The children's stories would have been different; their relationship to the world around them is different and would create other stories and other meanings.

Out of these mothers' stories, a narrative has emerged about The Mother's Room of flight and exile. It is a narrative about conflict and division, but also a narrative about strength and life. For in this room, women take care of the new life – and their children. This responsibility is a source of strength, but also of vulnerability in relation to those in power.

In this space, we also meet the sorrow of separation from the children. The mothers perhaps fought for a better society for their children, but many of them came to realize that the priority they gave to that struggle hurt their relationships to their children – and their children's relationship to the world around them.

6. The Living Room

During the time just after I came to Denmark, I met my husband again. We hadn't had much contact while I was in prison, only sent short letters to each other – so of course I talked with him about it. At that time I kept dreaming about being arrested. It was strange. I hadn't dreamt about it at all while I was in prison. But my husband and I trusted each other – also about sex – so when we met in Denmark, it was natural for me to talk to him about what had happened. (Latin America)

They finally met in exile's Living Room. It had been a long time since they had shared their daily life, and during this time, she had experienced life in The Cell. Their relationship was strong enough to bear the separation, as well as the story of what had happened in The Cell. After arriving in the safety of exile, however, the anxiety returns in nightmares, an anxiety that she could hardly allow herself to notice while she was undergoing the experience. Their relationship must also contain this trauma of the past.

In the homeland, she went out into the public space and was wounded. She was especially vulnerable, because she *also* had a life in the private sphere as a woman with a husband and children. Having a husband, just like having children, is a source of special strength and special vulnerability. In the space of The Cell, such vulnerability can be exploited, and by concentrating on her sexuality, her children and her relationship to her husband, those in power will teach her to stay in her proper place. However, if the confidential space – the basic trust – between her and her husband can be maintained all through the structural and organized violence, then that vulnerability can perhaps also be turned into strength.

I am still in love with him. I don't think there is another woman who loves her husband like I do. I worry about him. I am sad when he is sad. I won't have him suffer any evil – never, never. I love him more than at the beginning. It is the best thing in my life. I feel strong because of him, and he feels strong because of me. We always think in the same way. But it isn't good for us here. My husband just stays at home. He isn't old, only 50 years old. If he was in his own country, he would still have work. (Middle East)

But to maintain the loving relationship in the Living Room of exile seems to be difficult. Many exile marriages break up, although no systematic investigations have been made on the subject. Swedish studies show, for example, that the divorce rate among Latin American refugees is far higher

than the Swedish divorce rate (Agger & Jensen 1989). Among the women in
The Blue Room, ten out of 18 women from the Middle East who lived with
their husbands had difficult or significant problems, and one-tenth of the
whole Middle Eastern group was divorced. Among the Latin American
women, seven out of eleven who lived with their husbands also had difficult
or significant problems in their relationship, and more than half of the
whole group was divorced (Agger 1991).

> My husband very much wanted us to come to Denmark. Two years had
> passed since we had seen each other. I was only 23 years old when we were
> separated. When I saw him again in Denmark, I was terribly shocked. He
> was so changed. It was as if he had become rigid. At home he had been a
> lively and active person, but when we met here, he had become
> completely without feeling. We couldn't talk about it. He has relaxed a
> little now, but he still has problems. He has lost everything he had: his
> good job, his home. (Middle East)

The identity conflict between life in the private and public spaces, this
conflict which we have already met in The Daughter's Room and The
Mother's Room, is found again in The Living Room of exile. Here, we also
meet the split we encountered between parents and children, but now we
find it to be between woman and man. It is a conflict and split produced by
factors both outside and inside the relationship. In The Living Room of exile,
the external and internal factors become interwoven to such a degree that it
is difficult to differentiate between those that come from outside, from the
public space, and those that come from inside, from the private space. This
impenetrable tangle of outer and inner factors probably contributes to the
difficult problems and the dissolution of so many exile marriages.

For the woman who was politically active in the homeland, it can be
difficult to find a way to continue her activity in The Living Room of exile
unless she can join with other women in the same situation.

> Then we started learning Danish. At the same time, we were very active in
> solidarity work. We learned Danish because we wanted to tell Danes
> about what was going on in our country, not because we wanted to stay
> here. We weren't thinking of getting an education or studying anything
> here. (Latin America)

The woman who was not politically active herself, but who chose to
follow her husband into exile, can experience a forbidden anger toward her
husband, the one whose 'fault' it is that she is in exile, even though she
'ought' to stand by him. In exile it can be detrimental *not* to go out into the
public space. The space of exile itself is public. If she does not acknowledge

the political quality of exile, but tries to transfer life from the private sphere in the homeland to The Living Room of exile, she will lose an important means of overcoming the feelings of both complicity and shame arising from the conditions of exile. For example, exile can mean a decline in social status for her husband, who now 'just stays at home'. If he succeeds in getting work, however, the transition to The Living Room of exile can be less of a problem.

> I was in a Latin American women's group and I found out that those who had the fewest problems here were the housewives. They had lived as housewives in the homeland, and they hadn't been especially active politically. They came here with their husbands and children. They had everything with them. When they came to Denmark, there was no question about their identity. Here, they would also be housewives and take care of the problems at home. So they had only to move their homes here. But girls like me, who didn't have children or who came here as single mothers, had big identity problems. (Latin America)

The relationship can be influenced by the conflict between her political consciousness and desire for liberation, and her relationship to a man who represents the structural oppression of an androcentric society. Furthermore, this conflict can be called forth by the traumas from the space of The Cell, which one or both carry with them when they arrive in The Living Room of exile.

> Our relationship came under pressure after we came to Denmark. I don't know if it was because of my husband's experiences from prison and torture or it was the exile situation. He wouldn't talk about what he had been through in prison, but I think it affected him in that he didn't believe in other people. He didn't even believe in himself. He went to apply for work an awful lot of times, and I used to say: "Good luck, I'm crossing my fingers for you. Remember to be yourself and talk slowly and clearly and show them what you can do." But he felt like a loser even before he had gone out of the door. I can't give him all the blame. I must also have done something wrong. But he felt that he had lost his political identity in Denmark, and that was why the only thing he wanted was to return to our country. It was one of the big problems between us. The day after he finished his studies he said: "Shouldn't we go home?" I asked, "What about my education?" We both studied, and I also had a right to finish my education. "Okay, when you are finished, we'll go home." Seven years went by, and he never got a job so that I could work less and have time to finish my studies.
> During the first years, we both studied and had the same

opportunities. We were lucky enough to be able to send our children to nursery school. But then I got the idea of getting a full-time job so that he could have more time to study, instead of borrowing money from the bank. It would be better for one of us to finish. So we did that. I got a job in a kindergarten as a substitute for a support teacher. I guess I did all right, because I was offered a permanent job. In the meantime, my husband finished his education and I began to study again, little by little. My husband still couldn't find a job. It was humiliating for him, especially what the others said about him. When I wasn't home, he cooked, washed up and took care of the children. But as soon as I came home I had to take over. And he couldn't accept it, if I was together with my colleagues after work for example. He became jealous. "You're not to act like Danish girls!" he said. And you can't imagine all the negative things he could say on such occasions. It was his opinion that Danish girls were too liberated. But the problem was that he couldn't remember that when I had been studying at the university in our homeland, I also went out with my classmates. We didn't go to bars, but we went out to eat at a café. That was okay, but then of course I didn't live with him. I think he would have accepted it if he'd had the same opportunities himself. But he didn't experience the things I experienced, and he also needed someone at home he could talk to.

So little by little, problems arose. We ended up getting divorced two years ago. But why didn't he trust me? I can't figure out whether it was because of all the things he had experienced or if he just *was* that way. But it is certain that the relationship you have to a sweetheart at home is completely different from what you experience living together in Denmark and getting married. (Latin America)

During this process, whereby their behaviour patterns increasingly diverge, the one becomes more and more isolated while the other becomes more and more outgoing. The one who is isolated has in this case also been traumatized by torture and is forced to receive all the positive and identity-strengthening feed-back from the outgoing member of a relationship that becomes more and more antagonistic. A power struggle develops which limits the possibility of their building together a creative and outgoing system which they can share.

The sum of all these factors, which exist both inside and outside the relationship and weave themselves together and mutually influence each other, can result in this split between them. The political struggle against the external system emerges as a private struggle between the two within the relationship's system and makes it difficult to maintain a loving relationship. At the same time, the private trauma can *also* emerge as a sexual–political struggle between them.

Arrivals

It seems as if there is not really any joy connected with arrival in The Living Room of exile. If only it was a little warmer outside. But it isn't. It is cold, and people rush by.

One day I sat in the bus and a woman came and sat beside me. "Where do you come from?" she asked me. I told her. "I don't know that country," she said. I explained to her that the situation was very bad in my country, that there was much war. "But why did you come to Denmark? We already have so many refugees here," she said. "Why didn't you go to another country?" I didn't answer. When I came home I cried, and my husband asked me what had happened. "I don't know," I answered. But it is not my country, and the people ask me why I have come to Denmark. I hope that war is finished soon. Then I will hurry back. (Middle East)

Yes, no doubt about it – it is foreign territory, and the welcome is rather cool. Perhaps it is difficult for love to thrive in the midst of this cold and alien place. But how could it be – this arrival in exile? Arrivals can present opportunities: for the relationship to develop and be consolidated, but also for it to become completely different.

I came to Denmark as a refugee when I was 17, and I married my sweetheart when I was 18. Then I became pregnant. I had never tried to live together with a man, have my own money, manage everything. And I had to manage a love life at the same time. My husband was also very young, and the Danish girls here. . . . He was no male chauvinist. He was a middle-class fellow, and very conscious in a way. . . . He learned the language quickly, and he didn't have all the problems I had. He had been on his own for several years. He hadn't been at all protected by his family as I had been, so he could take care of himself. He began to go out alone, and I was pregnant and alone at home a lot. I went around with my big stomach, and I was still just a girl myself. I needed my mother, very much. And I cried a lot. Everything was new for me, and there was no one who could tell me what being pregnant was all about. How it was that the baby kicked. I had simply never talked with my mother about these things, or with anyone else. I became pregnant because of this emptiness. What should I do otherwise? I felt bad, and had no desire to contact anyone. I went around the apartment and talked to myself. He played guitar and Bob Dylan and all that, and he was very popular and lively and intelligent. He also kept active politically and became acquainted with some Danish people. When I had the baby, he went to Germany to work, and of course he had a good time, too. I stayed behind alone in the apartment. I couldn't speak Danish. He was away for a half year, and also found a German girl. He didn't send any money, so I had to manage alone. But then he moved back after all, even though I had thrown all his things out over the balcony. I couldn't stand it. It was too much. It went up and down with our relationship. I really loved him, looked up to him, idealized him. He was the only one for me, and he was also all that I had here. I couldn't stand the idea of leaving him, even though it was awful for me that he had others. Every time he came back, I just said "yes". I guess we had a love–hate relationship. He must also have been dependent on me, and loved me. We had known each other since we were 15, and we had such big dreams about our relationship, our children and our future. We shared a dream world. But we had also grown up together. He was the first boy I went to bed with. It was very beautiful for both of us. It was a very idealistic relationship we had then. We were influenced by the 1968 movement. So it was more than just leaving each other. It meant also giving up all our dreams. So he always came back, and I always took him back. And it was good and it was bad. It was mostly me who felt bad. But I always took care of my child. She was never hungry or abandoned. No, that was all I had in my mind, that my child was my responsibility. My parents and my upbringing had given me that much strength: I knew that I had to manage that. There was no strength left for myself, but there was just enough for the child. (Latin America)

Like many other exile stories, this story of arrival ended in divorce. It is a love story in which both try to maintain their political engagement, their dream of another world. But for her, the conditions outside The Living Room of exile manifest themselves as an inner conflict, and a split between them that is reinforced by circumstances they brought with them. This is an impenetrable conflict, almost impossible to resolve, of a relationship which is destructive within the private sphere, but at the same time is experienced as the only link to a political identity. Rather than helping support the link to this identity, arrival in exile reinforces the experience of being separated from the public space. It is almost as if you must create that separation yourself in order for the relationship to survive:

I'll never forget the three months in refugee camp. We had one room, and we had to live with 300 other people. We felt awful. Everyone felt bad, not just us. Everyone was unsure about the future. No one knew what to expect. So they couldn't be kind to each other. We lost our patience about the smallest things. We got mad at each other, and things like that. I almost never went out of my room, because I had to take care of my little baby. I didn't feel like talking to anyone, either. (Middle East)

To arrive as a refugee seeking asylum is only a partial arrival, and during the waiting period a strategy for survival must be found. Within the limited physical space allotted to the family, it tries to establish its boundaries in relation to an undefined world outside. But the walls are thin.

> From the camp, we were sent to live on a ship. Those were bad times. Very bad times. I have tried to forget that time, but I can't. Sometimes I hate Denmark because of that time. In the camp, I was fine, but on the ship we were about 2,000 people, and each family had only one cabin. You could hear everything that went on in the other cabins. There were many children, and often they didn't sleep until after one or two in the morning. They were noisy and we were tired. We were there for about three months. We were given asylum after 50 days . . . Only they forgot my daughter, so we had to wait another two months until she was given asylum. Finally, the Red Cross helped us, and the police apologized to us. They had forgotten her papers. When we came under Danish Refugee Aid, they put us up at a hotel in Copenhagen's red-light district. We lived there for four months. There was only one bath and one toilet for 30 rooms. We asked to be moved from there, and they found us a house that we had to share with three other families. Finally, we found a good house for ourselves, and we live there now. It's nice — it's our own house. (Middle East)

Sluzki (1979) points out how important it is to have some host families to receive refugees at the time of arrival; they can act as substitutes for the extended family that is such an important part of life in the homeland. In this way, the arrival could be 'ritualized' in a process that might be able to prevent the family system's disintegration. But unfortunately flight is 'a transition without any or very few known rituals' (Ibid. p. 382). Usually, refugees are left to suffer the painful process of exile with only the help of their own private rituals.

> In the beginning, after arriving in Denmark, it was difficult. We were like prisoners. But gradually we became more mature – we also received help from a much older couple who arrived with us. They were just like our parents. They were also from our country, but they have returned home now. We lived with them for a while, and received the help we needed. We were lucky. Otherwise, we would probably have left each other. (Latin America)

Daily life

For those who had been politically active in their homeland, participation in the struggle for a better society was an important part of their sense of identity and thus their connection to a meaningful context. Being a creative member of a group is an important defence against the dictatorship's system of oppression (Barudy 1988). Continuation of the political engagement in exile, however, is not necessarily sufficient to maintain a loving relationship. The love relationship must exist within a new and very different family system. Just like other external stress-producing events, exile causes radical changes in the family system's internal structure. Even though family systems are dynamic and constantly changing, too great changes can be difficult to embrace.

After arrival in The Living Room of exile, changes take place within the whole of the family system: a new assignment of roles and responsibilities is required; new boundaries and a new division of power have to be defined; new forms of communication must be established; new rules agreed upon; new ways to handle closeness and distance in the relationship must be found; and the family system must be flexible in relation to these changes (Agger & Jensen 1989). Sharing the housework, for example, can be a serious and new area of conflict if there were servants in a family's previous life together. Well-educated, middle-class women who come to Denmark have to manage without the servant girl who made it possible in the homeland to have a job as well as manage the home and children.

The sociologist Diana Kay (1987), in a study of Chileans in exile in Britain, discovered that exile increased the well-educated women's experience of repression in their marriages. Power struggles arose in connection with renegotiation of roles, responsibilities, boundaries and sharing of power in their relationships. The women could not accept having responsibility for all the functions in the home while they were working or studying.

The marriage didn't hold. He couldn't stand my independence. It wasn't a question of economy. We each already had our own economy in our homeland. Even though I earned less than he, I always had my own money. But he couldn't tolerate my need to move around and be independent, also my work. He has always been very unsure of me for some reason I can't explain. He claimed that I didn't love him enough. I got to feel that I had so many roles: taking care of the children, taking care of the house, taking care of him – I was also his sweetheart and his mistress. I also had to do my job, and I needed a little time to myself. Finally, I was completely exhausted. A day has only 24 hours. I couldn't manage it. So the marriage actually disintegrated after ten years. He couldn't adjust to the fact that we had no servants. In my homeland, when both the man and wife work, they have a servant girl. But you can't do that here. He didn't help at all at home. My job was exciting, but it wasn't anywhere near as exciting as his. That was more important for him. He worked all the time. He is that type of man who throws himself into his work, body and soul. So I was at work for eight hours, and then I went home and took care of the kids and the washing, the shopping and everything. And every time I said anything about it, he'd say: "I can't do it just now. I'll do it tomorrow or the day after." He never took it seriously. At the same time, he was very jealous. Now, if I had been a woman who had three men . . . but I never gave him any reason to be jealous. He suffocated me and said he loved me and loved me. Finally, I said I wanted peace. Peace. I didn't want another man. I simply wanted peace. He took it very hard, and I have also had a bad conscience about what I did to him. Now I feel reasonably good about my life, I think. (Latin America)

In this case, she chose to leave a relationship that was not flexible enough to adjust to the daily life in exile. In the conflict between life in the public and private spaces of exile, she chose the life of a single woman. According to Kay's study, many middle-class women make the opposite decision. They feel that they have to give up their studies or their work because they have lost their servants. Working-class women, however, have lost the support they received from the extended family's network. For both groups, the result is that they feel more repressed in their marriages: they feel ill, anxious, and guilty about breaking with what they have learned about the right way to act in a marriage. Many housewives feel isolated and lonely in their homes. They have their husbands and children with them, but they cannot compensate for the loss of the extended family's network and the neighbourhood fellowship.

This whole process that started with the meeting with the world of exile contributes to a *politicizing* of the relationship between the man and the woman: 'Exile opens up for a re-evaluation of the woman/man relationship', Kay says (1987, p. 195). We could say perhaps that an invisible pattern becomes visible. The context changes so much in exile that you are forced to see the hidden patterns in order to be able to create new rules for the relationship.

Sometimes I talk to my husband about it, that I don't like being a housewife. I don't know why. Maybe because I sometimes see other women who have problems with their husbands. Maybe that's it. As a young girl I dreamt about loving a completely special man. (Middle East)

Sexual rebellion

Sexuality is part of the relationship, and through the sexual communication between the couple, boundaries can be either defined or violated; power can be exerted; roles and the responsibility for the sexual relationship can be assigned; rules defining the 'right' way can be established and maintained more or less rigidly, and intimacy or distance can be created.

> Among the women here from my country, there is a lot of talk about women's satisfaction. Earlier, they didn't talk much about that. I think it plays an important part in marriage problems. There are many women who are not satisfied with their sex life. Therefore, they have problems with their husbands. Earlier, because of our traditions, you couldn't show it. There was absolutely no discussion about it. Outside the bedroom it was forbidden to speak about it, so women kept these problems to themselves. But now there is much discussion that this is also a kind of repression. Why shouldn't a woman also be satisfied with her sex life? We discuss this a lot in my organization, and many of the divorced women have told us that their only problem was their sex life but that they had never talked about it before. It was the women who decided that they should be divorced, because they were not sexually satisfied, and they couldn't do anything about it. So they got divorced. (Middle East)

Maybe a woman can have problems with her husband because their sex life is unsatisfactory. Maybe she has sexual problems with her husband because the *relationship* is unsatisfactory. The sexual relationship is a sensitive barometer for the dynamics in the marriage system. At the same time, sexual weapons have a special wounding quality.

From the space of The Cell, we know that sexual weapons can strike at such deep and unconscious levels that it is difficult to defend oneself against them. And inside the sexual area of a love relationship, power struggles can be fought and territory claimed in a hidden and almost unconscious way. Both sexes can use sexual weapons in the power struggle, but usually they do it in different ways: while the man mostly expresses power demands and hate through potency without tenderness, the woman can express her power (or her rebellion) in an apparent lack of sexual desire (Schmidt, 1989).

The women in the story above used perhaps the most effective sexual weapon if they wished to escape from a repressive relationship. But the sexual problem can also be a way of defending oneself against a conflict that is far too threatening to deal with – the conflict between being devoured by one's partner, or being deserted:

I don't think I'm a normal woman. I'm abnormal in the sexual area in the relationship with my husband. Maybe I'm frigid. I am very cold. When we make love, I would like my husband to do a lot of things to get me ready. But I think most men think that's something women do automatically. My husband thinks that he is normal, and I am abnormal. We can't talk about it. My husband doesn't speak freely about his feelings. He keeps them inside him, but after a time suddenly they all come out, and he gets very nervous and angry about small things. And I understand that the anger is a translation of something he suppresses day after day. If I were a Danish woman, I would leave him immediately. But we have so many things that are more important than sex. Therefore, we choose to repress it and think about something else that is more important. I think it's like that for my husband. (Middle East)

In exile, the marginalized couple have only each other, and they can be forced to be so close that it can become intolerable. In the above account, to create distance one of them must make herself sexually 'frigid', while the other has to 'lock his feelings in'. Even in a completely ordinary relationship, not strained by exile, it can be difficult to manage too great a degree of intimacy. Schmidt has a possibly disillusioned, but perhaps also realistic concept of the sexual relationship in marriage. Intense sexuality cannot, he believes, be united with the intimacy of living together. Marriage 'does not tolerate intimacy or symbiosis in sexuality, but at best the distance in a sexuality that perhaps is just exactly comfortably satisfying. More is unbearable. . . . It is an absolutely necessary and reasonable protection of one's own autonomy and identity against being completely "dissolved"' (1989, p. 77).

In an exile situation, most of the couple's network, such as family and work, are cut away. There are few other spaces in which to enjoy emotional relationships; therefore, it is even more necessary to protect oneself against too intense intimacy with one's partner.

In a few stories from The Living Room, the sexual relationship has developed to the point of rape on the man's part. In the sexual political struggle between the two, the man reacts with this weapon against the woman's wish for more freedom:

When I got divorced from my husband, some didn't agree. But I did it because it was *my* opinion. Our relationship was bad because we didn't agree, and I didn't know him very well before we were married. We didn't have any nice times together. Earlier, I always thought that when I married, we would be very close, and if there were any problems we would sit down and talk about them. We wouldn't be angry at each other. But in our relationship it wasn't like that, because we were very different.

Even though he was also from my country, it was as if we were from two different societies. I couldn't accept his traditional attitudes. Ever since I was very young, I had fought for freedom. I was political, and therefore I couldn't stand living in a prison again. If my husband was a man who would make a prison for me, then I couldn't accept him. Maybe some other girls would be able to, but I wasn't like that. Therefore, there was trouble between us, and he did those things. I hate him. Also it was my first sexual relationship, and I had a bad experience. Now I have bad feelings because of the experiences with my husband. Before, when I saw a romantic film, it made me feel happy, but now I can't stand it. If I see, for example on television, a couple kiss each other, I feel strange. I think it must be a lie – it can't be right. It's only a film. If one day I got my feelings again, and a man came along whom I loved, I would like to marry again. But I probably won't. (Middle East)

Rape, of course, occurs not only among those in exile or from other cultures. In Western society too, social power relations manifest themselves especially brutally in sexuality: 'Every third second a woman [in the USA] is raped, in about half of the cases by someone she knows', says Schmidt (1989, p. 176). The fusion of power with violence and love with sexuality is widespread, however, and it can reveal itself in a complicated way in marriage, for exiles too.

The Latin American exile psychologists Corral and Paez characterize many exile relationships as 'sado-masochistic'. The marginalized and wounded man needs to be *seen*: in order for her to notice my presence, I make her suffer. But if he lets me suffer, I in return have reason to counterattack (COLAT 1980).

My sex life in marriage has been dominated by rape, rape, rape – and nothing that has anything to do with love. I didn't know that what I experienced was rape. I first found out about that when I went into therapy – that what I described was nothing other than rape. I thought that rape was something that happened in a dark, remote street in the middle of the night. I didn't know that it could also happen in a marriage bed. And if all Latin American marriages are like mine, then I can say that 90 per cent of the Latin American women have been raped. If not by others, then by their husbands. I had learned all my life that I should just do whatever my husband desired. It is only now, after I met my Danish boyfriend, that I have learned to say no. It was only with him I learned a concept of sex completely different from what I'd had before. He didn't really understand my reactions; they were something quite unknown for him. But I never had an orgasm with him. He was just sweet. I am alone now, and it is only now that I belong to myself. If I don't think about the loneliness, then I feel fine. By loneliness I am thinking of the longing for a real love life. (Latin America)

Let us close the door to The Living Room. We return now to The Blue Room with that feeling of yearning which is essential for any change. The narrative about the loving relationship in The Living Room of exile tells us about the continuous conflict between longing for love and the power relations which limit its possibilities of fulfilment.

7. On The Veranda

I am 34 years old now, and I feel that my life's dream is over. I feel like an old woman. I would so like to return to my country. Here in your country, relationships between people are not strong. (Middle East)

The door opens out onto the space of The Veranda. On the threshold, we turn and look back over the voyage through the rooms in the woman's house of exile. What did we discover on this journey?

We wanted to investigate how politically dangerous women were punished and controlled. Because sexuality plays a major role in this control and punishment, we also wished to investigate how this method of disciplining politically active women was connected with the existing sexual–political power structure and with the historically transmitted definitions of 'shameful' and 'impure'. We hoped thereby to deepen our understanding of the problem of *complicity*: the paradoxical feeling of being an accomplice that is experienced by a person who is abused. By understanding the social and psychological dynamics of this phenomenon, we hoped to be better able to heal traumata resulting from politically organized violence against women. But perhaps we would also deepen our understanding of the dynamics of sexual trauma in general and of the conditions for women in particular.

In order to investigate these questions, we have now journeyed backward in time and forward again into the everyday life of the present. But also, through an inner psychological process, we have moved down toward the darkest and most evil aspects of existence. During this process we have entered a series of rooms in a 'woman's house of exile', within which we have described these problems and examined their perspective.

Each of these rooms was a universe in itself within the female world of exile, but each of them also illustrated dimensions common to every woman's life. And in a woman's life, some of the most important definitional spaces are those having to do with sexuality and reproduction. It is mostly within these defining rooms, therefore, that the social and political control of women is carried out, the discipline of those dangerous women who do not wish to conform to what is expected of them – those who do not wish to be silent and invisible.

In an androcentric society, men are neither defined, nor define themselves, to the same extent as do women, in relation to their reproductive functions within the private sphere. Rather their definitional spaces are found within the sphere of production and the political–economic power structure. If women in such societies leave the private sphere and enter public space, speak out and become visible – for example through sexual or political rebellion – they can create a crisis in the system. This results in disorder and 'impurity', which represent an especially powerful threat against a society which is already in crisis. The visible women become dangerous women – both sexually and politically.

But when women in these societies leave their private houses, they also leave an important protective shelter. As 'public women' they become vulnerable, and can be wounded in a way that perhaps can never be healed. In spite of this, the narrative from The Blue Room is also a testimony about the *necessity* of rebellion and of moving frontiers in order to expand freedom of movement and fight the power of shame, even though this struggle means persecution, exile, and marginalization.

When I met the women in The Blue Room, I tried to give our conversations a dimension of testimony. In this way, it was sometimes possible for a healing process to develop alongside the actual research process. This possibility is inherent in the very concept of testimony: it provides both documentation and purification. In addition, the testimony method contains an element of ritual, since symbolically one can transfer the internalized evil to a sheet of white paper or into the therapeutic space: into a *healing circle* (Cienfuegos & Monelli 1983; Agger & Jensen 1990). As researcher, I was interested in developing more knowledge about my subject, and as politically engaged psychologist, I was interested in contributing to the efforts to give voice to an area that has been shrouded in taboo, to make it visible and create a way in which we can speak about the unspeakable. All these factors can have a therapeutic effect, since they are part of an effort to connect the private and political spheres. The research process in The Blue Room did, at best, have such healing aspects, and for the researcher, too, it could create a connection between the private, professional and political levels.

The first definitional space we met during our journey through the women's house of exile was The Daughter's Room. In this space, social control of the girl and young woman were symbolized through the ambiguous relation to her blood. This blood was an outward sign of the transition from one stage to another. The first menstruation, the girl's blood, marked the transition from girl to virgin, while the blood of defloration, the man's blood, marked the transition from girl to woman. The blood's arrival, or its failure to arrive, were warnings regarding status, social boundaries that had been crossed, and perhaps also social boundaries that had been violated. In this space, the girl learned about the shameful dangers that threaten careless people; one of the most serious dangers that threaten the careless is contamination or impurity. If there were no blood on the wedding night, it could be a sign that the girl had been involved in forbidden sexual acts. No matter how the forbidden act occurred, with her consent or against her will, she is an accomplice. She could have been more careful. It was her responsibility, it was she who should be careful not to bring shame on herself and her family.

In The Father's Room, we learned about the power of shame from another perspective. Here, we heard about violation of girls' sexual boundaries in the public and private space. The Father's Room symbolized the 'illegitimate' side of the structural violence of patriarchy – patriarchy that has trespassed its own boundaries. On the one hand, these violations of sexual boundaries can be seen as an expression of inherent contradictions in the social control of women's sexuality: she is considered both pure and impure, prostitute and madonna, human being and object of exchange. On the other hand, these violations can be seen as an indication that control has run wild and begun to undermine its own foundation. By transgressing the incestuous barrier, the very social and cultural foundations of patriarchy are violated. Nevertheless, it was the girl's responsibility, in the space of The Father's Room too, to be careful that such transgressions did not happen. It was her responsibility and shame, and she was taught this responsibility when she moved out into public, male territory. Here, there was a constant need to be alert and protect oneself against male transgressions. When such transgressions became incestuous and occurred within what ought to be the protective shelter of the private sphere, according to culturally transmitted patterns of meaning, the girl also discovered that she was responsible. She thought that she need not 'be careful' in the private sphere, but here also she was present in her ambiguity: as the pure and the impure, the daughter and the sexual object. Thus, she experienced not only shame, but also an attack on her basic trust in the world, and a confusion in her values.

From this space, we entered The Cell, where we encountered the evil which became the decisive turning point in this narrative about the woman's house of exile. Here, the woman also met the organized political violence carried on outside and inside the walls of The Cell. Many of the women had met structural, and more or less conscious, violence in the other spaces in various local forms. But the meeting with *conscious and systematic* violence is the particular experience that is the reason for exile and life in this woman's house. In the definitional space of The Cell, women were not only controlled as sexual beings, but also controlled and punished as political opponents. The methods of control and punishment used had the same dual character: she was dangerous because she had left the woman's space of the private sphere, entered male territory and become visible; she was also dangerous because she, perhaps in collusion with male comrades, had threatened the established political power. Within the walls of The Cell, in prison, she met the *political technology* of the woman's body and, in this political prison, they sought to marginalize and mark her. Torture was supposed to disgrace its victim by disgracing her body, and the political technology of torture consciously exploited gender differences. Therefore, the means to disgrace the woman's body could be inspired by the methods of control already known from The Daughter's Room and The Father's Room. These methods were morally violating and could elicit feelings of complicity, impurity and shame that rendered the woman powerless as a political opponent. The power of shame had been internalized throughout her development and life in The Daughter's Room and The Father's Room, and could therefore be incorporated into the technology of torture used against her body. And when she returned to life outside The Cell, the humiliation would follow her: she could have been more careful; she could have been more alert; she could have resisted more – maybe she even invited the rape herself. Her status as woman could be changed from pure to impure. She therefore had to keep what happened in prison as a shameful secret. If her secret were revealed, it could cause not only her social death, but her political death too. The inner demoralization and the social humiliation had thereby fulfilled the aim of the systematic and conscious violence: to break the will and command obedience.

From The Cell, we entered a new definitional space of women, The Mother's Room. This space was defined by the consequences of organized violence for the mother–child relationship. Responsibility for the child is one of the 'female priorities' which she is assigned by society, and a task which she also takes upon herself. The 'new life' is something of value of which she must also 'be careful'. Political persecution had violated her bodily boundaries and affected both pregnancy and birth. The evil could penetrate so deep inside her body that, after the sexual violations in prison, she could be filled with doubt as to whether she would give birth to a child or a 'monster'. The violence also penetrated deep into the dynamics of the mother–child relationship. The woman experienced herself as an accomplice in the traumatic consequences for her children. She could perhaps have been more careful; she could have been more alert. Within this space, she experienced the conflict between a woman's priorities: her responsibility to take care of the home and give and nurture life, and her political engagement, which in the short-term threatened or destroyed her potentialities to fulfil this responsibility of womanhood. Seen in a longer perspective, political engagement was perhaps necessary, if she were to have any possibility of providing the kind of life she wished for her children. This inner psychological conflict was enacted in exile, where she could also experience a split between herself and her children. They could be divided by her wish to return to the homeland and the children's wish to remain in the country of exile; by her wish to remain in a marginal refugee position and her children's wish to 'belong' and be integrated. This division was accompanied by yet another inner psychological conflict: if she were to follow her children's wishes, then her political struggle would perhaps have been in vain. Maybe she would be closer to her children, but her life would have lost an important part of its meaning, the engagement that was the reason for her exile.

The visit in this room led us naturally enough into The Living Room, which is defined by the relationship to the present or absent husband and father of a woman's children. This relationship could be a source of both strength and vulnerability. Could the relationship bear the story of what happened in The Cell, or did she have to keep her secret? It was a secret that could become an 'obsessed' area in their relationship: if she told about it, she risked being deserted; if she didn't tell, she violated their confidential space. Apparently, it was difficult to maintain a loving relationship in exile. In The Living Room of exile, the outer and inner factors became interwoven in a way that makes it difficult to differentiate between what came from outside and what was internal. And in this space, the relationship was also affected by her identity conflict between a life in the private and the public space. We also re-experienced the split, but here between woman and man: exile's political problem could become a private problem between husband and wife.

In this space, we met an everyday life that caused radical changes in the inner structure of the family system. These changes could be accompanied by power struggles and privatization of external problems. In exile, the family was cut off from most of its network: no family, friends or work. The marginalized couple were left to themselves, and thus could be forced into an intimacy which could become unbearable. In addition, in the country of exile, they were confronted with new and different opportunities for women. This could give rise to sexual rebellion by the woman, who wanted more freedom, against the man, who tried to maintain control over the family. This rebellion could result in violence on the man's part and sexual violation of wife and children. Often, this rebellion led to divorce, and the refugee woman had to learn to live as a single woman and mother. In this new life, she could experience another conflict: on the one hand, a yearning for a loving relationship; on the other, her experience with male structural and political oppression.

A central theme for all the rooms in the woman's house of exile was the identity conflict that dangerous women can experience when they choose to leave their life in the private sphere and move out into political space and challenge male power, when they are not careful and contaminate the system by violating some of its boundaries. One penalty could be that *their* boundaries were violated.

All the women of The Blue Room had been wounded in their bodies and souls by their meeting with political violence, this extreme expression of the structural violence of patriarchy. In their efforts to expand gender boundaries, move the limits for what was permissible and fight against the power of shame, they had met evil. The imperative rebellion left them wounded by traumata that can never be fully healed.

Rituals and healing

When the physical body is wounded, it begins to heal itself in a process which can be either supported or obstructed. When the psyche suffers serious trauma, it will unconsciously attempt to heal itself in more or less appropriate ways. This is a healing process which can be supported, both by the conscious part of the 'self' and by the structure of which the self is part or chooses to be a part. The traumatized individual can choose to place her/himself in a context which supports a healing process.

During this journey, I became increasingly conscious of the healing significance of purification rituals practised in group contexts with different local variations. Within most psychotherapeutic theory, it is not common to regard the therapeutic process as ritual. It is true that catharsis is spoken of as a means of purification, but this does not have the symbolic significance to be found in many cultures' purification rituals. In any case, the mystical or magical element is, in theory, of subordinate significance in common psychotherapeutic theory. But which factors are actually active in the healing of psychological trauma?

Frank (1973, pp. 2–3) has attempted to summarize the characteristics present in all psychotherapy, both in industrialized societies and in other cultures: we have an educated, socially recognized healer, whose healing power is acknowledged by the sufferer and the social group to which he or she belongs; we have a sufferer who seeks help from the healer; and we have limited and more or less structured series of contacts between the healer and the sufferer, through which the healer, often with the help of a group, tries to induce specific changes in the sufferer's emotional state or in his or her attitudes or behaviour. All those involved believe that these changes will be beneficial. Although physical or chemical means can be used, the healing power is primarily practised through words, actions and rituals in which the sufferer, the healer and the group (if found) participate together.

The group can be included in the process as in group or family therapy, but it can also be part of the world outside and structured like a consciousness-raising group, or for example, like the grassroots groups within the Chilean human rights movement. In the latter case, the group will be its own 'healer' (Agger & Jensen 1993b).

According to Frank's definition, which I find quite precise, *belief* is an important ingredient in a therapeutic process. The sufferer must believe in and trust the therapist, and the therapist must believe in her or his own healing abilities. But to our thinking, 'belief' does not have high scientific status, and many theorists of psychotherapy have tried to eliminate any mystical or magical aspects of the profession in order for psychotherapy to be considered a respectable scientific discipline. To this end, many efforts have been made to measure the effect of psychotherapy and find the relationship between results, the therapist's training and experience, and the method used.

Psychologist Esben Hougaard (1989a; 1989b) has summarized in two articles a long series of these studies, and he reaches the following provoking (for therapists) conclusion: even though it can be documented that psychotherapy *works*, it is not yet possible to find evidence that the result is related to the therapeutic method employed, length of treatment or the therapist's training or experience. The effective factors are rather to be found in 'non-specific' elements such as the patient's belief in the therapist, and the therapist's personality, enthusiasm and confidence in own methods. Although these results can be due to weak investigatory techniques, they do present, as all good research should, important questions about the many dogmas within common psychotherapeutic theory and methods.

From a rational, 'European', scientific point of view, it is a disagreeable conclusion, which could undermine the existing psychotherapeutic power structure. But instead of repudiating this conclusion as a result of questionable research methodology, we could choose to see where it leads us. Frank believes, for example, that it is these non-specific factors that are effective in therapeutic processes throughout the world, whether they be healing rituals of tribes, religious revivals or European psychotherapeutic treatment. Even though, according to Hougaard, there is no direct 'evidence' that Frank is right, no one seems to have been able to prove him wrong.

It can be difficult for psychologists and psychiatrists who have been trained within a specific scientific discipline to accept that belief can be a more important healing factor than the therapist's training. But if we turn to anthropology, then this way of thinking is not so foreign.

Anthropological theories about the ritual process, the pure and the impure, the fieldworker's meeting with foreign cultures and the significance of symbols are of general psychotherapeutic interest and of special interest for the understanding of sexual trauma and its dynamics. Such an understanding will also be significant for development of transcultural psychotherapeutic methods of treatment, and can contribute to a valuable understanding of trauma resulting from violence in our own culture.

I will briefly present some characteristics of that specific type of ritual process which anthropologist Victor Turner (1974 p. 196) understands as marking the transition from one state to another, the so-called *rites de passage*. These rituals can be of a healing nature, or they can mark other forms of change, for example, the transition from child to adult. Taking his point of departure from anthropologist Arnold van Gennep's concepts, Turner has divided the ritual process of transition into three basic phases which characterize many types of rituals in various cultures: a *separation phase*, during which one is removed from ordinary daily life, a *threshold phase*, in which one is in an ambiguous state, midway between the old state and the new; a *reunification phase*, in which one is again united with the social structure, often on another level.

When we apply these concepts to common psychotherapeutic processes, we find that we also have a separation phase, when the sufferer (patient, client) is alone with the therapist. There is a threshold phase, when, in the therapeutic space behind closed doors, they work together on the sufferer's problem. The rules of communication here are different from those which apply in daily life. In the reunification phase, the sufferer is again a part of the customary environment, but now with an altered attitude toward the self and the others. These phases characterize both each session and the whole therapeutic process.

In the threshold phase, which Turner calls the *liminal phase* (limen = threshold), a feeling of fellowship can emerge. Turner tries to describe this feeling by the Latin word *communitas*. Communitas is central, for example, in various forms of artistic expression, in religion and in many social forms of the 'subculture'. We could add that it is also central in a successful psychotherapeutic process. Here, the old, limiting pattern can develop into a source of creativity through the relationship between the therapist and the sufferer. In this relationship, factors such as transference and counter-transference processes, empathy and the therapist's ability to embrace and reinterpret the trauma story are of significant importance for the healing process of the threshold phase.

The content of the threshold phase is difficult to define (and Turner used many words and years of his life in the attempt), but it could be characterized as an experience of inner transformation (Turner 1990). In the feeling of fellowship in the threshold phase, deep emotional layers are contacted by the help of symbols that vary from culture to culture. In this phase, conditions could arise for what Frank might call *kairos*; a state in which a person becomes ripe for basic changes in values and attitudes. But seen 'from outside', the threshold phase is ambiguous, because in this state one finds oneself in a social 'no-man's land' where one no longer necessarily follows the commonly accepted rules for good behaviour. In this state, on the one hand, one enters a 'tunnel', to use one of Turner's expressions. One cannot know where the tunnel will lead and it can be dark and frightening.

On the other hand, it is on the way through this tunnel that one can encounter the new and challenging.

The kind of social ambiguity characteristic of people who find themselves in the threshold phase can also be found in other groups. But then this ambiguity is not part of a process that aims at reunification with the social structure, but rather a permanent state. This applies for example to many participants in the consciousness-raising groups of the women's movement, and also to political refugee groups in exile in our countries. There is no immediate solution to the ambiguity of the consciousness-raising group or the refugee group. According to Turner's definition, they are *marginal* groups (margin = edge, limit, boundary), because they belong at one and the same time to several different social groups with contradictory norms. The women in consciousness-raising groups rebelled against a male-dominated society and lived that rebellion, while at the same time, they had to continue living on the edge of this same society (unless they decided to drop out and live in women's communities). Refugee groups live with their cultural background on the edge of the culture of the country of exile, unless they try to 'forget' their background and become part of our culture or drop out and live in ghettos. And refugee *women*, who in their homelands rebelled against the traditional male culture, find themselves in a doubly marginal position, since they are also in opposition to the ordinary social definitions in their own culture. The refugee group's rebellious women, and some of them have told their stories in The Blue Room, thus represent marginality's antagonistic ambiguity in an extreme form, with the possibilities which that position 'on the edge' also provides for insight that can transcend boundaries.

On the inner level, such a marginal state is experienced as a painful identity conflict, but the ambiguous position can also be a point of departure for deeper insight. Turner points out that it is in exactly such marginal groups that we find people of highly developed consciousness, who have been able to exploit their situation to develop new thinking and artistic creativity. This point of view is confirmed by the new scientific and artistic ideas which the women's movement brought with it. The Latin American exile sociologists Ana Vasquez and Ana Maria Araujo (1990) emphasize that exile also provides an unexpected opportunity for professional and political development. Marginality or ambiguity is, therefore, not something which absolutely should be 'treated'. That first becomes necessary when the identity conflict becomes so overwhelming that it can no longer be contained or when the controlling or punishing power strategies used against the rebellious marginal group have such a traumatic and violating character that individual members of the group or the whole group are overcome by despair, feel powerless or demoralized.

Subjects such as sexual oppression in childhood and marriage were central in the work of the basis group. The reason for discussing these subjects was primarily political: by gaining more knowledge of these aspects of women's lives, new forms of resistance could be developed against sexual oppression, against structural violence. But it was unavoidable that just touching on such subjects, which for many women were traumatic and partly repressed, could open old wounds that needed healing. Many times the groups were completely unable to handle the strong feelings triggered by these subjects, and the group would develop a dynamic that was destructive rather than healing. But under favourable conditions a healing process could emerge that was not planned but happened almost as a kind of side effect. Since experiencing this, I have been occupied with trying to understand exactly what caused the healing process to work.

I believe that the most important element in this healing was the systematic use of testimony as a working method. The use of testimony, during which the individual told her private story about a common oppression, was partly a form of purification and partly a de-privatization of the individual's emotions. This method nurtured the feeling of fellowship, or *communitas*, on a deeper level. The testimony method was thus part of a common ritual process that for a time changed the marginal position full of conflict, to a healing fellowship of the threshold phase. I believe that this aspect of the work of the consciousness-raising groups made it possible to continue a creative life in the borderland of marginality when the meeting was over.

The use of testimony is known not only from the work of the women's movement. There are many anthropological narratives from widely different parts of the world that tell about purification rituals which rid one of inner evil by bearing witness in the presence of a socially recognized person or the whole society in a culturally recognized context (Agger & Jensen 1990). The use of testimony is also central to self-help groups such as Alcoholics Anonymous. To transform the feeling of being guilty and impure, to 'make the ugly beautiful' is one of the most important themes for victims of violence, whether it is the silent violence in the family, incest, rape or organized political violence.

When the need for absolving oneself of such feelings arises or when the identity conflict becomes so overwhelming and leads to demoralization, then we need to search for the healing qualities of the ritual threshold phase. One must leave, for a time, the ambiguity of the marginal state, and separate oneself from its conflicts by entering the threshold phase's *purposeful* ambiguity, together with other members of this persecuted minority group. Refugee women in exile in the West must perhaps isolate themselves from that world for a time and go off with other refugee women in order to permit a healing process to begin. To remain in the borderland of the marginal state indefinitely can reinforce demoralization.

After such a ritual separation, the refugee woman will perhaps be able to be reunited with the marginal state on another level. She will regain energy to utilize that position's opportunities for creativity and insight. Women from the consciousness-raising groups did not need to relinquish their insistence on another kind of woman's life, and the refugee woman does not need to be 'integrated' in Western society in order to escape the marginal position's conflicts, but perhaps they must go off for a time and go through a healing process.

We will therefore go off for a time. We step over the threshold to yet another room in the house and come out onto a Veranda with a view. In this space, I attempt to invent and define a context in which insight and experience can begin to be connected to the healing process of the group. In this space, I search for that feeling of fellowship, that *communitas* which accompanies the healing qualities of the threshold phase in ritual.

I imagine how complicity, ambiguity, impurity and shame can be made visible, be voiced and given name; how a healing circle can be created which can contain both engagement and integrity – and despair and demoralization; how insight and understanding can take root and grow; and how the women can then rise and continue the journey – together or each one separately. On The Veranda, the marginalized group leaves for a time the ambiguity of exile which is so full of conflict.

A healing circle

It is late afternoon, and almost time to say goodbye. The colour of the light has changed. The weather has cleared and the afternoon sun reaches us. The narrative of The Living Room is still with us. The voice speaks of *dreams* and *yearning*. The voice carries us along as we step over the threshold and out into this space. One after another they come out and sit together in a circle. The researcher sits in a corner outside the circle. They know that she can hear their words, but they must create their own fellowship. The light filters through the green plants that grow up around the windows of The Veranda. Here it seems a bit chaotic and there is an atmosphere of desertion. It is as if this space wants to be given form and be inhabited. Old dreams flicker about and try to find a way out. Maybe a woman sat here once with a child and wished that they were not so alone. Maybe a girl once looked out of the window here and dreamed of justice.

> I felt as if I lived in a glass cage, where people understood what I was saying but I just couldn't hear them or understand them. Maybe I understood the words, but I couldn't understand the meaning behind the words, the system. It was so terrible – to want to get out of that glass cage.

It was like an invisible wall that you must get through in order to be with the others, but you can't find out how to get through. . . . Now there's no wall any more. I was in therapy, and it was only afterwards that I could cry. It turned out I was able to cry very violently. That helped me a lot. And – I just want to survive. At one point, while I lay in bed with anxiety – it is simply indescribable – that psychic state that made me physically ill – then I thought: "How can I refuse to allow the soldiers to destroy me as a person?" And at one point I found out that no matter what it cost me, they would not break me as a human being. So that's my personal victory. (Latin America)

To survive, then, it was necessary to build a glass wall against the destructive aim of those in power. It was necessary not to understand the meaning of their words. Then that flimsy glass wall had to be replaced by a bulwark to protect the weakness they must not find. Afterwards, it becomes difficult to tear the wall down again, but it is necessary to do so, because behind it is a tidal wave of anxiety, anger and chaos. But dammed up behind it is also a life energy that is felt as a yearning for form and unity.

The voice of yearning from The Living Room spoke about a dream of a loving relationship. It is a dream about belonging, on a level completely without words, that lies deep within us and gives form and meaning to the frightening chaos. Douglas (1970) tells about longing for a ritual form of communication that has almost been lost. The dream of a fellowship, without words, expressed in symbols. And in the circle on The Veranda, the word would be passed in a search for this silent belonging that can encompass chaos.

If I go back, maybe I can't survive. The situation is so completely confused. I don't wish to jump into the fire and kill myself. Even if I did want to kill myself, I would do it in a more peaceful way. To go back now would be like throwing myself in the fire. But I would be ready to do it, if I knew it would bring peace. If I could do something that would bring peace, I would leave. But now they need people who are tougher than I. My time comes when they want peace. But it is a very deep trauma to see it and not be able to do anything. I try to repress it. Because if I keep reading the newspapers from my homeland, I get so depressed. Then I can't function right. I can't do my work. I also have to take care of my children – they are about to free themselves. My husband will also have his own feelings. So therefore I want to limit it. I wish to shut the door on something that gives me so much pain. It takes my strength without my being able to solve it. (Middle East)

But the door will not be shut. Fresh oxygen keeps fanning the fire that threatens to burn her up. Her political engagement can maybe burn her private life to ashes. But the children want to free themselves, and the husband wants to have his own feelings.

Loneliness would emanate from her in the space of The Veranda, but also the warmth from her fire. Her dream about being together, belonging and bringing peace would perhaps spread out into the circle – the desire to belong to the world, to feel oneself as part of a larger pattern that connects all living things (Bateson 1988).

One is idealistic enough to believe that human beings are the best we have in the world. Man can do unbelievable things. Man can travel to the moon. The worst part was to lose my belief in other people. It's also because one is so idealistic. In any case, I believed that I was doing something for other people – make a better society, more just without so many class differences, so that all people had the chance for something better. And suddenly you met the others, the torturers, they were like people from another world. I had always been so proud, so maybe that's why it was such a hard blow for me. I can't stand someone humiliating me. I would almost rather die. The worst wasn't that they maybe hit you or gave you electric torture – I feel that was nothing compared to the way they undermined you as a person. I never, for example, allowed a man to touch me if I didn't want him to. But you just had to accept everything. I cry now, but I couldn't allow myself to cry then. You know what? Not a tear fell from my eyes then. Maybe it would have been good if I had cried, because maybe then they would have showed me some mercy. But of course, there were others that cried and they didn't show any mercy. But I was so angry. I felt such great hatred. I think that's what saved me. I think that if I could have, I would have killed right there. (Latin America)

She would look at the women who spoke before her. For a moment which she would not forget, the ice of mistrust formed by her meeting with 'the others from the other world' melted. Then she had to defend herself with pride and hatred against the chaotic void where everything falls apart, becomes insane or dies. With the ice, she gave chaos form.

The power-holders have *their* way to try and create order, by using terror. It is a strategy that leads to hierarchically organized units in deadly balance (Antonovsky 1987). But a constant process toward disorder and chaos is the earmark of all living things. The power-holders do not acknowledge this. It is a pervading myth, and not only among dictators, that disorder and rebellion can be opposed by exerting power in a way that compels fear. But the order thus created is deadly. And in the circle of The Veranda, what had been frozen would begin to melt as a warning that a new life-giving disorder was on its way.

The weapon of terror of the disappearances was the worst. One is paralysed forever. You keep holding on to the few things you have left, and if you are to hold the rest of the family together, you have to be very careful. I don't think I can do anything to get over it. Maybe it could have helped if I had stayed in my country, because then you meet so many in the same situation. But from one day to the next you suddenly have nothing. You have no house, furniture. And suddenly you have to pack in that confusion. All the important papers – my son's birth certificate etc., the whole file of papers I didn't take with me. But I took my wristwatch that my father gave me when I was 15. And I took a tape-recorder which was the last thing I bought together with my husband. They were strange things, and I wasn't conscious of it. I don't know why I took such things. It is very strange what you're like when you are in a borderline situation. If anyone asked me the day before, what I would take with me, I would have answered that I would take money and important papers, underwear and those kind of things. But I didn't do that. I had a mixture in my bag of many strange things. For example, I went out of the house to get two bathing suits that hung on the line. What was I going to use them for? It was completely crazy. (Latin America)

How can she say goodbye to someone who has 'disappeared'? The mourning process cannot be concluded, and she is left in unending paralysis and stagnation in the wake of chaos. But would he who disappeared have wanted that, the others in the circle would ask: such paralysis is the very purpose of this disappearance, because it prevents dangerous political activity. They wanted you to always 'be careful' and never threaten them any more.

It would begin to get dark outside, and they would light a candle on The Veranda. The next woman would face the circle and begin her testimony about the same unending sorrow and about the yearning she no longer dares listen to.

I am still angry with the military and the police. It hurts that they haven't been properly punished. I think it is worst for all of us who know someone they have killed. And also with all that destruction, that things haven't changed. I can never feel happy after losing my husband, but if things were more just, it would be some comfort. Then I could see some meaning in it. But it is as if everything has been meaningless. Because there are still so many people that die of hunger, and so many children that die of disease. They don't get medicine and they live on the street. And it doesn't look like it will ever change.

I have completely lost my political engagement. I think it's because I received a shock that I haven't overcome. I lost so much, and that always follows me. The only thing I did, when I first came to Denmark, was to join a women's group. It was a help. It was nice to do something that wasn't dangerous and be together with other people. And I also talked about things in that group that I never had talked about before. I have also talked with my new husband about it. It is obvious that you never can have the same relationship. The new relationship is different. The relationship I had with my husband was my first love, and we grew and developed together, were active together. So there were many things – and I'll never have such a relationship again. Never. Also because then I gave myself 100 per cent and actually lost. Therefore, I have to keep a little for myself. And if I went into a relationship 100 per cent again, and he died – what should I do then? Should I be able to begin again? (Latin America)

She would look at the others in the circle and they would recognize her 'never'. The loss of love is felt as a personal failing and has remained as mistrust – they would also feel that toward each other, here on The Veranda. The trauma has created chaos in the foundation of basic trust, and she has come to doubt whether the world has anything good for her; whether the world is meaningful; and whether she has any value. Her clear realism would also spread through the group and formulate important questions on fundamental assumptions about the world: is it wise to give oneself completely? Can one's life have meaning in ways other than through political engagement? In what ways am I meaningful for you?

The next one in the circle would say, 'Maybe you could also listen to my story'.

My husband disappeared, and I lived illegally until I was able to come to Denmark. Four years later, I learned that he had been killed. He had been taken by the military and sent to a concentration camp where he died under torture. But it was not an official message. I learned about it through a book with lots of information collected about former prisoners. It was terrible. It is still terrible. I don't believe you can ever get over it. It is simply inhuman. It is always difficult to accept that one you love is dead. But if you are together when it happens and can say goodbye and cry together, and if you can come with flowers every day to the same place, then you gain a kind of inner peace.

It took a long time before I could tell my son about the things that happened. I did that for the first time about two years ago, and now he is 13. So it took a long time. Before, he thought that his father died of a heart attack, but he had a suspicion. He always asked me lots of questions about it, but he was also careful, because he could feel that it was a subject I couldn't really talk with him about. It took me a long time, but I felt an urgency about it, because he would soon enter puberty and would begin to have many other conflicts with himself. But it was nice, beautiful and liberating, to cry together with him and talk about it. Now I can talk about it all right, but when I do, it is like a book I have read. It is like a story. When I hear myself tell about it, I think, "Do you understand that it's you?" (Latin America)

Also now, while she tells her story to the others, she would show her sorrow. The story is at the same time real and unreal. Part of it must be kept at a distance like a book she has read. She has to take care of herself so that she does not drown in the horror of it. But the group on The Veranda would be able to contain her story and meet it with that empathy which is a necessary and defining ingredient of the therapeutic attitude (Kohut 1990). As a minimum, the self that has been fragmented by deliberate and systematic abuse needs to meet the empathy of the therapeutic group. Here on The Veranda, empathy would become possible because her world is not foreign. Here the *solidary relationship* could emerge, the non-neutral relationship which is a therapeutic necessity for work with trauma following political violence (Weinstein, Lira and Rojas *et al.*, 1987).

The first three years I lived in another country, only my body was there. A big part of me, three-quarters of my brain, lived in my homeland. I read the newspapers like crazy. I wanted to hear news from everyone coming from there. I actually still lived there. I missed and missed and missed my country. But *missed* isn't the right word. I was filled with the desire for revenge. That was all I could think about. For the first time in my life, I wished that I could kill. At the same time, I felt enormously guilty about my sweetheart being murdered. Because it was me the police were looking for, not him. Then gradually I started to understand that the hatred I felt only hurt myself. It was something that happened inside me. It didn't have any effect on the police or the dictatorship – only on me. And then it slowly disappeared. But before that, I couldn't get away from that feeling. It had power over me. But it took much longer to get over the feeling of guilt. That was completely different, because it was me they had been looking for. (Latin America)

Guilt over surviving while the others are dead. Everyone in the group would recognize that, each with her own variation. It is a feeling of complicity that makes it morally wrong to feel good in the house of exile. It is a feeling that makes the one who is persecuted responsible for her own persecution.

The longing for 'the good' and the internalized 'evil' remains an inner conflict. This conflict is felt as an unbearable anxiety.

Sometimes I think that I simply cannot live. I don't belong, not in Denmark or in my country. So where shall I be? I have the feeling that I'm not anything. It has been much too hard. It is not only leaving my country; my life also broke into pieces. I was interrupted in my development from child to adult. I often feel guilty: I ought to have chosen to stay, like my father said. Rationally, I know it is the fault of those in power, but when I cry and feel badly, I feel that I ought to have stayed. I go around with lots of conflicts. For me, being a refugee is punishment. I can't see it any other way. I survive, but it is a hard sentence. I have been punished now for 15 years. I get permission now to return, and I return and can't work it out. And I say: "Damn it, how can they keep on with this punishment?" I feel that I'm destroyed for life. I will be a foreigner forever – both here and there. (Latin America)

She can feel herself only by relating to another person, but will she ever dare approach a trusting relationship, or will she always make herself a stranger to others? What is it that the living, human system 'learns' when it is subjected to conscious evil?

The experiences I had the first month I was under arrest were really hard. I don't like to talk about what happened, because I feel that what was most important for me was the time after I was transferred to the concentration camp. We were only women who had all been subjected to about the same things. So we talked a lot about what we had experienced, because we all shared it. And I think that's what has helped me most to stand the things done to me. We talked a lot, and we laughed a lot, even though that might sound a bit strange. It was as if we could make all the horrible things we had experienced meaningless, because we could see them from above. I think most of the women I was together with in prison got along all right afterwards. We talked a lot about sexuality, because they use mostly sexual violence. But I think we realized that a love relationship is something completely different, that you can forget the bad experiences. You feel dirty, of course. You can't get away from that. It is difficult to remove the filth from your body. But I believe what helped most of us best was the "gossip therapy" we had in the concentration camp. I was with the other women for five months, when we could speak with each other openly. I think that was the best therapy I received. I didn't know the other women earlier, but we were all from the same party and we had mutual friends. We quickly came to a deep understanding of each other. I still have contact with them and we have great confidence in each other, even though we were together for only a short time. We were all afraid – we felt the same. But I don't really know how it started, how conscious it was. At first, you just want to forget those experiences, shut them out. You think maybe that if you talk about them, you will live through them again. But I think we talked them to death. We talked so much about our experiences that we didn't need to talk about them any more. (Latin America)

She would look at the woman who spoke before. 'You can get over it,' she perhaps would say. 'You can use us. You can make all the horror that has happened to you meaningless, if you see it from "above" and connect it with its political significance.'

There would still be some experiences she would not want to give words. The shame would still have retained some of its power. It is hard to remove that impurity from the body, even though the group of women in prison talked about it and realized that a love relationship was something entirely different. Her shame would be felt in the circle on The Veranda as a form of modesty that would make it difficult to continue or to ask her more questions. It is a shame that cannot be removed with words alone. But empathy and fellowship are purifying. And she would continue:

I think there will always be some small wounds afterwards. For example, I get so tense whenever I go for a gynaecological examination. Even though it all happened so many years ago, and even though I have a fine woman doctor. I also sweat too much. But in general, in almost 98 per cent of my life, I have overcome the experience of prison. (Latin America)

Even though her body is afraid, she understands why it happens. She does not drown in the chaos. To react physiologically, as she does, is not uncommon. After being subjected to traumatizing events, you can react spontaneously, physically, when you are in situations which resemble the trauma (Ochberg 1988). The body remembers what another part of the system, the consciousness, has 'forgotten'. The body and the 'brain' cannot be separated. They are one comprehensive, dynamic system. But she has not yet been able to integrate the anxiety and shame into that comprehensive whole in a meaningful way. We can therefore find 'unconscious' physical and emotional reactions, at the same time that the conscious part of the self experiences having recovered from the trauma.

Different levels of the dynamic system are reacting. From a classical Freudian point of view, it is an important part of the therapeutic process to make the unconscious conscious. But this point of view only considers part of the functions of the unconscious, the part which stores memories full of repressed anxiety and pain. But we can also look at the unconscious from the viewpoint of learning. In this area, the *unconscious* carries out functions which it would be most inappropriate to be conscious of. We are unconscious of much of what we have learned: it has become a habit which we act on automatically. And 'the better an organism "knows" something, the less conscious it is about its knowledge. . . . Such habits sink to deeper and deeper levels of the mind' (Bateson 1972, p. 134). It is essential for survival that this is possible.

But if the learning process has been very 'thorough' and carried out under traumatic conditions, some 'habits' that are injurious to the individual's relationship to her or his body, self and surroundings can sink to such deep, unconscious levels that they can perhaps be reached only through means of ritual.

The next woman in the circle would add her story about what her body had learned.

> I was raped and things like that. It seems as if I have overcome it. Now, I can see that it didn't have anything to do with me. They tell you that you're a whore. And it was well known that I wasn't married when I had my first child. You don't do that in my country. They had that information and they used it against me in a terrible way. And I didn't know where my child was either. It was only later that I learned that she was with my parents. But everything having to do with sex, that's something you would rather not talk about, and that can well be the reason that I never talked with my first husband about what happened to me in prison. Because that would awaken all those feelings it maybe wouldn't be necessary to awaken. (Latin America)

But her body remembers, the living system remembers. The feelings that she does not wish to awaken would come to life here in the healing circle. She would continue by reflecting about what she learned then, lessons of such an overwhelming nature that it is hard to 'unlearn' these habits:

> But there must be something or other about me that makes me always leave a relationship. It is always me who leaves. Except for the first time, I have always known, even if I was very much in love with the guy, that it couldn't last. Some way or another I feel that I won't fight for the relationship any more. I am afraid to stay in it. I run away. When problems come, I run away. When things get to be too much, then it's out. I can't continue like that. There must be some problem that makes me do it all the time. I don't finish things. Before I am finished, I run away. Repress the whole thing, just leave and start over again. It's not satisfying. I can't live in the same place for very long either. I begin to panic. During the 15 years I have been in Denmark, I have lived in twelve places. And every time I think: "Now I'm going to relax. Now I'm going to stay." But I can't. The longest I have lived in one place is two years. At

some point, I get that feeling: "Now I must get out." And sometimes it has been really stupid, because I have lived in some really nice places. But it is my own private exile. (Latin America)

There would now only be one woman left before everyone in the circle had given their testimony. She would lay her doubt and her lost political engagement inside the circle as yet one more document and yet one more piece of evidence.

In my homeland, I was very involved. I had a dream. It was as if my life had meaning, and it wasn't just something individual. But here in Denmark, I only decide for myself. If you don't have any cause, any dream, then it becomes an individual struggle. I am now trying to find my individual dream – it is no longer collective. And of course I also have children, and I think about their future. But we human beings need a dream, a goal for our lives, for otherwise life has no meaning. (Latin America)

Their voices would continue to put into words, to name. In the meantime, the researcher would get up and stand by the window. Everyone, both the women she met and she herself, were 'local editions' of what it meant to be a human being and a woman. They created a meeting point in the common space that emerged in testimony about the oppression that they had struggled against. They each contributed to this testimony from their specific backgrounds and from the relationship which was created during the meeting. In this relationship, the researcher was also her own informant, and she noted how she was affected, and sometimes overwhelmed, by the meeting with violence and conscious evil. As a psychologist and therapist, she also had some experiences that made it possible to relate consciously to the situation. This created an opportunity to hear the strong and liberating content in the women's testimony.

Through the women's testimony from exile which *she* – the therapist – wrote down, she presents documentation and evidence, documentation of the methods that those in power use to control and punish dangerous women, and evidence that perhaps can be used in the fight against those in power. With this political message, she attempts to contribute to the struggle for respect for fundamental human rights.

On the way, she received new knowledge about how the power of shame can be used to control and punish; about childhood's gradual internalization, in the feeling of shame, of the power outside, and about how this feeling is connected to how we understand what is pure and impure. She saw how the impure person can be made by the others to feel an accomplice to her own contamination: she could have been more careful; she could have taken care. And she also saw how the impure one can make herself responsible. When the others hurt her, it must be because she is herself evil. The evil must correspond to something inside herself, if nothing else then to not being careful. She saw how it was part of life in the social structure always to be careful that forbidden boundaries are not violated; and how the development of an inner power of shame contributes to creating obedient, silent and invisible women. Those who refuse to be obedient, but go out into the political sphere, are again struck by the power of shame. The political prison and its torture use the stamp of 'whore' as the special humiliating strategy against the woman's body, and the researcher saw that strategy as an extreme variant of the control-and-punish methods that women already know from childhood's internalization of the power of shame.

She described the psychological trauma of political violence with terms such as 'mistrust', 'despair' and 'demoralization', and she saw how this trauma forced its way deep into the woman's body and affected the unborn child and later the birth. She saw how the power of shame affected the relationship to the growing child and remained as an inner conflict in the woman, between her identity as mother and her identity as political activist. And she saw how the trauma also forced its way into the relationship to her husband and made it difficult for her to realize the yearning for a loving relationship.

She tried to create some healing spaces; she built a symbolic house in which the traumatic experiences could be told and receive new meaning. In these spaces, the trauma could be retold in its political context, and the shame could be returned to the system to which it belongs. She saw this as a beginning of a revision of the historically transmitted patterns of meaning that define the pure and the impure, the permitted and the forbidden. And she saw how a traumatic experience can lead to insight, to rebellion, to greater wisdom about life.

She finally summarized the therapeutic aspects of the different rooms of the house in the form of a healing circle. In this circle, she was present only as researcher. She could also have participated as therapist, but that was not the purpose of her project in The Blue Room. In the healing circle, each one put the traumatic and the ugly, and the evil, into the centre of the therapeutic space. Here, they began to see the private suffering from outside and to transform shame into political dignity – for the circle also creates a purifying space that is held together by the empathetic relationship between its members. It is a fellowship strong enough to also contain the evil.

In this space, they begin to experience the necessary turning point between the wordless nothing dominated by chaotic anxiety and the wordless fellowship given form and expression in the symbol of the circle and its healing ritual. It was a turning point that was passed almost without their being conscious of it.

What the researcher learned about the power of shame, about the pure and the impure, belongs not only to foreign cultures in distant lands. In our highly industrialized society, women are also subjected to violation: these forms of control are part of the structure of male society. In the West, too, the victims of incest, rape and wife battering feel that they are accomplices and impure, and that they could have been more careful, that they could have taken better care; and, too, it is their responsibility that others do not violate their sexual boundaries. The basic mistrust of the world and one-self, despair and demoralization are also terms which can describe their traumata. In their healing process, the power of shame must also be taken seriously. New rituals must perhaps be developed, rituals which can absolve their feeling of impurity. But that would be a new research project – or a new clinical practice. For the women who are marginalized in the women's house of exile, it is especially urgent to understand how this house is a part of the larger pattern. The rebellion and suffering are connected to conditions which also exist outside the universe of the house.

On The Veranda, the women are about to depart. They rise, and while they put on their coats and shawls, they say their goodbyes. They say a friendly goodbye to the researcher and go out into the borderland of exile. Perhaps they are on their way home; perhaps they must remain refugees for a time yet. If necessary, they might come by and meet again on The Veranda. The researcher must also depart. It is time to go home. She blows out the candle and tries to take leave of this house. A long time has passed since she first stepped over the threshold into The Blue Room; a long time since she came here to write her narrative about the discoveries she made on her voyage. She collects her papers and takes her bag over her shoulder. Even though she has written her narrative, it still remains a part of her.

Afterword

This book could not have been written without the forty refugee women who trusted me enough to tell me their stories in The Blue Room. I can only hope that my narrative will contribute to bringing them justice.

I met with the women in connection with a research project carried out at the Institute for Cultural Sociology, University of Copenhagen, in 1988–90. I am grateful to The Danish Medical Research Council for providing me with the economic support necessary to realize the project.

While the book was being written, I had discussions with colleagues and friends whom I wish to thank for their interest and their helpful comments. Thanks especially to Søren Buus Jensen, Jonathan Schwartz and Susan Whyte for their support and challenging inspiration. I am, of course, responsible for the way their comments have been used in my narrative.

I want also to express my gratitude to Mary Bille for her conscientious work in translating The Blue Room into English, and to The Danish Literature Information Centre and The Danish National Commission for UNESCO for their financial support for the translation.

Inger Agger
Aalborg, Denmark

February 1993

Bibliography

Agger, I. (1977) *Basisgruppe og Kvindebevidsthed* (Rap Groups and Women's Consciousness-Raising) Munksgaard, Copenhagen.
—— (1987) 'The Female Political Prisoner: A Victim of Sexual Torture'. Paper presented at the 8th World Congress for Sexology, Heidelberg, 14–20 June.
—— (1989) 'Sexual Torture of Political Prisoners: An Overview', *Journal of Traumatic Stress*, Vol. 2, 305–318.
Agger 1991
—— (1991) Appendix 1, in 'Kvindeligt vidnesbyrd fra exilet' (Feminine testimony from exile). University of Copenhagen, Ph.D dissertation.
Agger, I. & S. B. Jensen (1989) 'Couples in Exile: Political Consciousness as an Element in the Psychosexual Dynamics of a Latin American Refugee Couple', *Sexual and Marital Therapy*, Vol. 4, 101–108.
—— (1990) 'Testimony as Ritual and Evidence in Psychotherapy for Political Refugees', *Journal of Traumatic Stress*, Vol. 3, 115–30.
—— (1992) 'Human Rights and Post-Traumatic Stress: The Human Rights Movement as an Important Factor in Prevention and Healing of Severe Trauma Following Human Rights Violations', in K. Achté, M. Henriksson, M. Ponteva *et al.* (eds) *Traumatic Stress – Psychology and Psychopathology* Psychiatrica Fennica Supplementum, Helsinki.
—— (1993a) 'The Psychosexual Trauma of Torture', in J. P. Wilson & B. Raphael (eds) *International Handbook of Traumatic Stress Syndromes*. Plenum Press, New York.
—— (1993b) 'Trauma and Healing Under State Terrorism. Human Rights and Mental Health in Chile During Military Dictatorship: A Case Example'. Unpublished report to The Council for Developmental Research, The Ministry of Foreign Affairs, Aalborg University, Denmark.
—— (in press) 'Determinant Factors for Countertransference Reactions Under State Terrorism', in J. P. Wilson & J. Lindy (eds) *Counter-transference in the Treatment of Post-Traumatic Stress Disorder*. Guilford

Press, New York.

Amnesty International (1991) *Women in the Front Line: Human Rights Violations Against Women*. Amnesty International Publications, London.

Andersen, M. H. (1992) 'Women in Politics – a Case-Study of Gender Relations and Women's Political Participation in Sukumaland, Tanzania'. Unpublished PhD thesis, Institute of Development and Planning, Aalborg University, Denmark.

Antonovsky, A. (1987) *Unraveling the Mystery of Health*. Jossey–Bass Publishers, San Francisco.

Ardener, E. (1989) 'Belief and the Problem of Women', in M. Chapman (ed) *Edwin Ardener: The Voice of Prophesy and Other Essays*. Basil Blackwell, Oxford.

Ardener, S. (1987) 'A Note on Gender Iconography: The Vagina', in P. Kaplan (ed) *The Cultural Construction of Sexuality*. Tavistock, London.

Barudy, J. (1989) 'A Programme of Mental Health for Political Refugees: Dealing with the Invisible Pain of Political Exile', *Social Science and Medicine*, Vol. 28, 715–27.

Bateson, G. (1972) *Steps to an Ecology of Mind*. San Francisco: Chandler Press.

—— (1988) *Mind and Nature*. Bantam Books, New York.

Bateson, G. & M. C. Bateson, (1987) *Angels Fear. Towards an Epistemology of the Sacred*. Bantam Books, Toronto.

Bidou, P. (1982) 'On Incest and Death' in M. Izzard & P. Smith (eds) *Between Belief and Transgression*. University of Chicago Press, Chicago.

Boscolo, L., G. Cecchin, L. Hoffman, & P. Penn (1987) *Milan Systemic Family Therapy – Conversations in Theory and Practice*. Basic Books, New York.

Brun, E. (1991) 'Livsformsteorien og den Dobbelte Rationalitet' (The Theory of Praxis and Double Rationality). Unpublished paper, Center for Feminist Research in Aalborg, Aalborg University, Denmark.

Bustos, E. & L. R. Ruggiero, (1986) 'Latinamerican youth in exile. Is it a lost generation?' Paper presented at the International Seminar of Centres that attend Refugees, 8–11 May, Frankfurt/M.

Carli, A. (1987) 'Psychological Consequences of Political Persecution: The Effects on Children of the Imprisonment or Disappearance of their Parents', *Tidsskrift for Norsk Psykologforening* (Journal of the Norwegian Psychological Association), Vol. 24, 82–93.

Cienfuegos, J. & C. Monelli, (1983) 'The Testimony of Political Repression as a Therapeutic Instrument', *American Journal of Orthopsychiatry*, Vol. 53, 43–51.

Clifford, J. (1986) 'Introduction: Partial Truths', in J. Clifford & G. E. Marcus (eds) *Writing Culture*. University of California Press, Berkeley.

CODEPU (1989) 'The Effects of Torture and Political Repression in a

Sample of Chilean Families', *Social Science and Medicine*, Vol. 28, 735–40.

COLAT (1980) *Asi Buscamos Rehacernos*. Celadec, Bruxelles.

Cox, M. & A. Theilgaard, (1987) *Mutative Metaphors in Psychotherapy*. Tavistock, London.

Douglas, M. (1966) *Purity and Danger*. Routledge & Kegan Paul, London.

—— (1970) *Natural Symbols: Explorations in Cosmology*. Barrie and Jenkins, London.

Ekman, K. (1990) *Knivkasterens Kvinde* (The Knife-Thrower's Woman). Samleren, Copenhagen.

Engdahl, B. E. & R. A. Eberly, (1990) 'The Effects of Torture and Other Maltreatment: Implications for Psychology', in P. Suedfeld (ed) *Psychology and Torture*. Hemisphere Publishing Corporation, New York.

Forest, E. (1985) 'Mujer y tortura' (Women and Torture), *Egin*, 6 March, p. 16.

Foucault, M. (1979) *Discipline and Punish: The Birth of the Prison*. Penguin Books, London.

Frank, J. D. (1973) *Persuasion and Healing. A Comparative Study of Psychotherapy*. The Johns Hopkins University Press, Baltimore and London.

Geertz, C. (1973) *The Interpretation of Cultures: Selected Essays*. Basic Books, New York.

—— (1983) *Local Knowledge: Further Essays in Interpretive Anthropology*. Basic Books, New York.

Goddard, V. (1987) 'Honour and Shame: The Control of Women's Sexuality and Group Identity in Naples', in P. Caplan (ed) *The Cultural Construction of Sexuality*. Tavistock, London.

Hashim, L. S. (1990) 'A Survey of Sexual Harassment in Dar es Salaam', Unpublished report, Tanzania Media Women's Association, Dar es Salaam.

Hastrup, K. (1978) 'The Semantics of Biology: Virginity', in S. Ardener (ed) *Defining Females: The Nature of Women in Society*. John Wiley & Sons, New York.

—— (1986) 'Veracity and Visibility. The Problem of Authenticity in Anthropology', *Folk*, Vol. 28.

Hastrup, K. & P. Elsass, (1988) 'Incest i Tvækulturel Betydning' (Incest in a Cross-Cultural Context), *Nordisk Sexologi* (Nordic Journal of Sexology), Vol. 6, 98–107.

Heller, A. (1985) *The Power of Shame: A Rational Perspective*. Routledge & Kegan Paul, London.

Héretier, F. (1982) 'The Symbolics of Incest and Prohibition', in M. Izzard & P. Smith (eds) *Between Belief and Transgression*. University of Chicago

Press, Chicago.

Herman, J. L. (1988) 'Father–Daughter Incest', in F. M. Ochberg (ed) *Post-Traumatic Therapy and Victims of Violence*. Brunner/Mazel, New York.

—— (1992) *Trauma and Recovery. The Aftermath of Violence – From Domestic Abuse to Political Terror*. Basic Books, New York.

Hougaard, E. (1989a) 'Dodo–kendelsen i Psykoterapiforskningen I: Non-specificitetsantagelsen' (The Hypothesis of Non-Specification in Psychotherapy Research), *Agrippa–Psykiatriske Tekster* (Agrippa–Psychiatric Texts), Vol. 11, 85–104.

—— (1989b) 'Dodo–kendelsen i Psykoterapiforskningen II: Alternativer til Non-specificitetsantagelsen' (Alternatives to the Hypothesis of Non-Specification in Psychotherapy Research), *Agrippa–Psykiatriske Tekster* (Agrippa–Psychiatric Texts), Vol. 11, 147–68.

Jackson, M. (1987) '"Facts of Life" or the Eroticization of Women's Oppression? Sexology and the Social Construction of Heterosexuality', in P. Kaplan (ed) *The Cultural Construction of Sexuality*. Tavistock, London.

Jensen, S. B. (1992) 'Sexuality and Chronic Illness: A Biopsychosocial Approach', *Seminars in Neurology*, Vol. 12, 135–40.

Kaplan, H. (1974) *The New Sex Therapy*. Bailliere & Tindall, London.

—— (1983) *The Evaluation of Sexual Disorders. Psychological and Medical Aspects*. Brunner/Mazel, New York.

Kay, D. (1987) *Chileans in Exile. Private Studies, Public Lives*. Macmillan, London.

Khairi, S. (1982) 'Torture in Iraq: A Personal Testimony', in *Iraqi Women Under Baath Repression*. Iraqi Women's League, London.

Kohut, H. (1977) *The Restoration of the Self*. International Universities Press, New York.

—— (1990) *Selvets psykologi* (The psychology of the self). Hans Reitzels Forlag, Copenhagen.

Kordon, D. R. & L. I. Edelman (1988) 'Observations on the Psycho-pathological Effects of Social Silencing Concerning the Existence of Missing People', in D. R. Kordon, L. I. Edelman, D. M. Lagos *et al.* (eds) *Psychological Effects of Political Repression*. Sudamericana/Planeta, Buenos Aires.

Kutchinsky, B. (1980) 'Blodskam/Incest' (Incest), in C. B. Thomsen (ed) *Den Man Elsker* (The One You Love). Statens Filmcentral, Copenhagen.

—— (1985) 'Om Incestproblemets Udbredelse' (About the Extension of the Incest Problem', *Kriminalistisk Instituts Stencilserie*, Vol. 28, 83–99.

—— (1990) 'Child Sexual Abuse: Prevalence, Phenomenology, Intervention, and Prevention. An Overview'. Paper presented at the Ankara Conference on Child Abuse, June 1989 (revised 1990).

Lévi-Strauss, C. (1968) *Structural Anthropology*. Allen Lane, The Penguin Press, London.

Lifton, R. J. (1988) 'Understanding the Traumatized Self: Imagery, Symbolization and Transformation', in J. P. Wilson, Z. Harel & B. Kahana (eds) *Human Adaptation to Extreme Stress*. Plenum Press, New York.

Lira, E. (1983) 'The Chilean Experience in the Psychological Work of Political Repression and Torture'. Paper presented at the Torture Treatment Conference of Amnesty International in Wisconsin, October.

Lira, E. & E. Weinstein, (1986) 'La tortura sexual' (Sexual Torture). Paper presented at the International Seminar: Consequences of the Repression in South America. Its Medical, Psychological and Social Effects. Montevideo.

Marcus, G. E. & M. M. J. Fisher, (1986) *Anthropology as cultural critique: An experimental moment in human sciences*. University of Chicago Press, Chicago.

Marner, T. (1987) *Familieterapi. Milano metoden* (Family therapy. The Milan method). Hans Reitzels Forlag. Copenhagen.

Mathiasen, S. & S. Lützer, (1992) 'The Survivors. Violations of Human Rights in Tibet – Healing in the Tibetan Exile Community'. Unpublished report, University of Southern Jutland, Esbjerg, Denmark.

McCann, I. L. & L. A. Pearlman, (1990) *Psychological Trauma and the Adult Survivor*. Brunner/Mazel, New York.

McCubbin, M. A. & H. I. McCubbin, (1989) 'Theoretical Orientations to Family Stress and Coping', in C. R. Figley (ed) *Treating Stress in Families*. Brunner/Mazel, New York.

Mernissi, F. (1987) *Beyond the Veil. Male–Female Dynamics in Modern Muslim Society*. Indiana University Press, Bloomington.

Nielsen, B. G. (1991) *Seksuelle Overgreb Mod Børn i Familien* (Sexual Abuse of Children in the Family). Aarhus Universitetsforlag, University of Aarhus, Denmark.

Ocbberg, F. M. (1988) *Post-Traumatic Therapy and Victims of Violence*. Brunner/Mazel, New York.

Saadawi, N. el, (1980) *The Hidden Face of Eve*. Zed Press, London.

Schmidt, G. (1989) *Han, Hun, Den, Det. Om Sexualitet* (He, She, It. About Sexuality). Tiderne Skifter, Copenhagen. German edition (1986) *Das Grosse Der Die Das. Über das Sexuelle*. März Verlag, Herbstein.

Sluzki, C. E. (1979) 'Migration and Family Conflict', *Family Process*, Vol. 18, 379–90.

Staub, (1990) Chapter in Suedfeld 1990, *q.v.*

Stover, E. & E. O. Nightingale, (1985) *The Breaking of Bodies and Mind. Torture, Psychiatric Abuse and the Health Profession*. W. H. Freeman and Company, New York.

Suedfeld, P. (ed) (1990) *Psychology and Torture*. Hemisphere Publishing Corporation, New York.

Trepper, T. S. (1989) 'Intrafamily child sexual abuse', in C. R. Figley (ed) *Treating Stress in Families*. Brunner/Mazel, New York.

Turner, V. (1974) *Dramas, Fields, and Metaphors: Symbolic Action in Human Society*. Cornell University Press, Ithaca and London.

—— (1990) 'Are there universals of performance in myth, ritual and drama?' in R. Schechner & W. Appel (eds) *By Means of Performance. Intercultural Studies of Theatre and Ritual*. Cambridge University Press, New York.

van Geuns, H. A. (1987) 'The Concept of Organized Violence', in Ministry of Welfare, Health and Cultural Affairs (ed) *Health Hazards of Organized Violence*. The Hague: Centre of Government Publications (DOP).

Vasquez, A. & A. M. Araujo, (1990) *La maldición de Ulises: Repercusiones psicológicas del exilio* (The Misfortune of Ulysses: Psychological Repercussions of Exile). Editorial Sudamericana, Santiago, Chile.

Warburton, A. (1993) 'EC Investigative Mission Into the Treatment of Muslim Women in the Former Yugoslavia'. Final report to the European Council, Brussels.

Weinstein, E. & E. Lira, (1987) 'La Tortura' (The Torture), in E. Weinstein, E. Lira, & M. E. Rojas, *et al.* (eds) *Trauma, Duelo y Reparación. Una Experiencia de Trabajo Psicosocial en Chile* (Trauma, Mourning and Reparation, Experiences from Psychosocial Work in Chile) (33–91). Fasic/Interamericana, Santiago, Chile.

Weisæth, L. (1991) Personal Communication.

Willner, D. (1983) 'Definition and Violation: Incest and the Incest Taboos', *Man*, Vol. 18, 134–59.

Wilson, J. P. (1989) *Trauma, Transformation, and Healing*. Brunner/Mazel, New York.

Winnicott, D. W. (1986) *Playing and Reality*. Penguin Books, London.

Index